Praise for Onion Deli

A Collection of Onion Reci
Cookbook Delights Series-Bo

..."One of the most versatile foods in the world now has a book devoted to revealing its entire splendor. The ***Onion Delights Cookbook*** is brimming with hundreds of recipes, facts, and folklore, regarding one of the world's most flavorful vegetables.

Author Karen Jean Matsko Hood combines complete information on the best ways to utilize onions. Recipes range from soups and salads to appetizers, entrées, beverages, and desserts. Hood tops it all off with a dash of poetry to present a creative cookbook that is most satisfying.

Onion Delights Cookbook has INSTANTLY become one of my favorites!"...

Kimberly Carter
Publicist

..."***Onion Delights Cookbook*** has fascinating tidbits that will delight and entertain your family. With witty and factual information about onions, as well as more than 230 wonderful tasty recipes, this cookbook promises to delight the palate and tantalize the taste buds. Also included is an enormous variety of scrumptious onion recipes that promise to deliver a unique experience.

The history and poetry that is included will intrigue and enchant the senses while enjoying the prose."...

Mary Scripture
Graphic Designer

Praise for Onion Delights

A Collection of Onion Recipes
Cookbook Delights Series-Book 8

...Praise to ***Onion Delights Cookbook*** which has all the makings of a classic favorite. Now you too can prepare that dish that everyone wants the recipe for!

Author Karen Jean Matsko Hood presents a wide variety of delicious recipes. This book will serve you well through any event, every day or special occasion, even through a seven course meal.

Instead of the same routine, try something new and exciting!"...

Ed Archambeault
Spokane, WA

..."***Onion Delights Cookbook*** is not only a cookbook, but a wealth of information about the onion. It includes fascinating facts, folklore, history of onions, cultivation and gardening, nutrition and health, and poetry. It even includes information on onion types.

In addition to all this information it has a collection of over 230 recipes that are delicious, and will be enjoyed by your family and friends.

This is a great value for the price and makes a wonderful gift."...

Dr. James G. Hood
Editor

Onion Delights

A Collection of Onion Recipes
Cookbook Delights Series-Book 8

Karen Jean Matsko Hood

Current and Future Cookbooks

By Karen Jean Matsko Hood

DELIGHTS SERIES

Almond Delights
Anchovy Delights
Apple Delights
Apricot Delights
Artichoke Delights
Asparagus Delights
Avocado Delights
Banana Delights
Barley Delights
Basil Delights
Bean Delights
Beef Delights
Beer Delights
Beet Delights
Blackberry Delights
Blueberry Delights
Bok Choy Delights
Boysenberry Delights
Brazil Nut Delights
Broccoli Delights
Brussels Sprouts Delights
Buffalo Berry Delights
Butter Delights
Buttermilk Delights
Cabbage Delights
Calamari Delights
Cantaloupe Delights
Caper Delights
Cardamom Delights
Carrot Delights
Cashew Delights
Cauliflower Delights
Celery Delights
Cheese Delights
Cherry Delights
Chestnut Delights
Chicken Delights
Chili Pepper Delights
Chive Delights
Chocolate Delights
Chokecherry Delights
Cilantro Delights
Cinnamon Delights
Clam Delights
Clementine Delights
Coconut Delights
Coffee Delights
Conch Delights
Corn Delights
Cottage Cheese Delights
Crab Delights
Cranberry Delights
Cucumber Delights
Cumin Delights
Curry Delights
Date Delights
Edamame Delights
Egg Delights
Eggplant Delights
Elderberry Delights
Endive Delights
Fennel Delights
Fig Delights
Filbert (Hazelnut) Delights
Fish Delights
Garlic Delights
Ginger Delights
Ginseng Delights
Goji Berry Delights
Grape Delights
Grapefruit Delights
Grapple Delights
Guava Delights
Ham Delights
Hamburger Delights
Herb Delights
Herbal Tea Delights
Honey Delights
Honeyberry Delights

Honeydew Delights
Horseradish Delights
Huckleberry Delights
Jalapeño Delights
Jerusalem Artichoke Delights
Jicama Delights
Kale Delights
Kiwi Delights
Kohlrabi Delights
Lavender Delights
Leek Delights
Lemon Delights
Lentil Delights
Lettuce Delights
Lime Delights
Lingonberry Delights
Lobster Delights
Loganberry Delights
Macadamia Nut Delights
Mango Delights
Marionberry Delights
Milk Delights
Mint Delights
Miso Delights
Mushroom Delights
Mussel Delights
Nectarine Delights
Oatmeal Delights
Olive Delights
Onion Delights
Orange Delights
Oregon Berry Delights
Oyster Delights
Papaya Delights
Parsley Delights
Parsnip Delights
Pea Delights
Peach Delights
Peanut Delights
Pear Delights
Pecan Delights
Pepper Delights
Persimmon Delights
Pine Nut Delights
Pineapple Delights
Pistachio Delights
Plum Delights
Pomegranate Delights
Pomelo Delights
Popcorn Delights
Poppy Seed Delights
Pork Delights
Potato Delights
Prickly Pear Cactus Delights
Prune Delights
Pumpkin Delights
Quince Delights
Quinoa Delights
Radish Delights
Raisin Delights
Raspberry Delights
Rhubarb Delights
Rice Delights
Rose Delights
Rosemary Delights
Rutabaga Delights
Salmon Delights
Salmonberry Delights
Salsify Delights
Savory Delights
Scallop Delights
Seaweed Delights
Serviceberry Delights
Sesame Delights
Shallot Delights
Shrimp Delights
Soybean Delights
Spinach Delights
Squash Delights
Star Fruit Delights
Strawberry Delights
Sunflower Seed Delights
Sweet Potato Delights
Swiss Chard Delights
Tangerine Delights
Tapioca Delights
Tayberry Delights
Tea Delights
Teaberry Delights
Thimbleberry Delights

Tofu Delights
Tomatillo Delights
Tomato Delights
Trout Delights
Truffle Delights
Tuna Delights
Turkey Delights
Turmeric Delights
Turnip Delights
Vanilla Delights
Walnut Delights
Wasabi Delights
Watermelon Delights
Wheat Delights
Wild Rice Delights
Yam Delights
Yogurt Delights
Zucchini Delights

CITY DELIGHTS

Chicago Delights
Coeur d'Alene Delights
Great Falls Delights
Honolulu Delights
Minneapolis Delights
Phoenix Delights
Portland Delights
Sandpoint Delights
Scottsdale Delights
Seattle Delights
Spokane Delights
St. Cloud Delights

FOSTER CARE

Foster Children Cookbook and Activity Book
Foster Children's Favorite Recipes
Holiday Cookbook for Foster Families

GENERAL THEME DELIGHTS

Appetizer Delights
Baby Food Delights
Barbeque Delights
Beer-Making Delights
Beverage Delights
Biscotti Delights
Bisque Delights
Blender Delights
Bread Delights
Bread Maker Delights
Breakfast Delights
Brunch Delights
Cake Delights
Campfire Food Delights
Candy Delights
Canned Food Delights
Cast Iron Delights
Cheesecake Delights
Chili Delights
Chowder Delights
Cocktail Delights
College Cooking Delights
Comfort Food Delights
Cookie Delights
Cooking for One Delights
Cooking for Two Delights
Cracker Delights
Crepe Delights
Crockpot Delights
Dairy Delights
Dehydrated Food Delights
Dessert Delights
Dinner Delights
Dutch Oven Delights
Foil Delights
Fondue Delights
Food Processor Delights
Fried Food Delights
Frozen Food Delights
Fruit Delights
Gelatin Delights
Grilled Delights
Hiking Food Delights
Ice Cream Delights
Juice Delights
Kid's Delights
Kosher Diet Delights
Liqueur-Making Delights

Liqueurs and Spirits Delights
Lunch Delights
Marinade Delights
Microwave Delights
Milk Shake and Malt Delights
Panini Delights
Pasta Delights
Pesto Delights
Phyllo Delights
Pickled Food Delights
Picnic Food Delights
Pizza Delights
Preserved Delights
Pudding and Custard Delights
Quiche Delights
Quick Mix Delights
Rainbow Delights
Salad Delights
Salsa Delights
Sandwich Delights
Sea Vegetable Delights
Seafood Delights
Smoothie Delights
Snack Delights
Soup Delights
Supper Delights
Tart Delights
Torte Delights
Tropical Delights
Vegan Delights
Vegetable Delights
Vegetarian Delights
Vinegar Delights
Wildflower Delights
Wine Delights
Winemaking Delights
Wok Delights

GIFTS-IN-A-JAR SERIES

Beverage Gifts-in-a-Jar
Christmas Gifts-in-a-Jar
Cookie Gifts-in-a-Jar
Gifts-in-a-Jar
Gifts-in-a-Jar Catholic
Gifts-in-a-Jar Christian
Holiday Gifts-in-a-Jar
Soup Gifts-in-a-Jar

HEALTH-RELATED DELIGHTS

Achalasia Diet Delights
Adrenal Health Diet Delights
Anti-Acid Reflux Diet Delights
Anti-Cancer Diet Delights
Anti-Inflammation Diet Delights
Anti-Stress Diet Delights
Arthritis Delights
Bone Health Diet Delights
Diabetic Diet Delights
Diet for Pink Delights
Fibromyalgia Diet Delights
Gluten-Free Diet Delights
Healthy Breath Diet Delights
Healthy Digestion Diet Delights
Healthy Heart Diet Delights
Healthy Skin Diet Delights
Healthy Teeth Diet Delights
High-Fiber Diet Delights
High-Iodine Diet Delights
High-Protein Diet Delights
Immune Health Diet Delights
Kidney Health Diet Delights
Lactose-Free Diet Delights
Liquid Diet Delights
Liver Health Diet Delights
Low-Calorie Diet Delights
Low-Carb Diet Delights
Low-Fat Diet Delights
Low-Sodium Diet Delights
Low-Sugar Diet Delights
Lymphoma Health Support Diet Delights
Multiple Sclerosis Healthy Diet Delights
No Flour No Sugar Diet Delights
Organic Food Delights
pH-Friendly Diet Delights

Pregnancy Diet Delights
Raw Food Diet Delights
Sjögren's Syndrome Diet Delights
Soft Food Diet Delights
Thyroid Health Diet Delights

HOLIDAY DELIGHTS

Christmas Delights
Easter Delights
Father's Day Delights
Fourth of July Delights
Grandparent's Day Delights
Halloween Delights
Hanukkah Delights
Labor Day Weekend Delights
Memorial Day Weekend Delights
Mother's Day Delights
New Year's Delights
St. Patrick's Day Delights
Thanksgiving Delights
Valentine Delights

HOOD AND MATSKO FAMILY FAVORITES

Hood and Matsko Family Appetizers Cookbook
Hood and Matsko Family Beverages Cookbook
Hood and Matsko Family Breads and Rolls Cookbook
Hood and Matsko Family Breakfasts Cookbook
Hood and Matsko Family Cakes Cookbook
Hood and Matsko Family Candies Cookbook
Hood and Matsko Family Casseroles Cookbook
Hood and Matsko Family Cookies Cookbook
Hood and Matsko Family Desserts Cookbook
Hood and Matsko Family Dressings, Sauces, and Condiments Cookbook
Hood and Matsko Family Ethnic Cookbook
Hood and Matsko Family Jams, Jellies, Syrups, Preserves, and Conserves
Hood and Matsko Family Main Dishes Cookbook
Hood and Matsko Family, Pies Cookbook
Hood and Matsko Family Preserving Cookbook
Hood and Matsko Family Salads and Salad Dressings
Hood and Matsko Family Side Dishes Cookbook
Hood and Matsko Family Vegetable Cookbook
Hood and Matsko Family, Aunt Katherine's Recipe Collection, Vol. I-II
Hood and Matsko Family, Grandma Bert's Recipe Collection, Vol. I-IV

HOOD AND MATSKO FAMILY HOLIDAY

Hood and Matsko Family Favorite Birthday Recipes
Hood and Matsko Family Favorite Christmas Recipes
Hood and Matsko Family Favorite Christmas Sweets
Hood and Matsko Family Easter Cookbook
Hood and Matsko Family Favorite Thanksgiving Recipes

INTERNATIONAL DELIGHTS

African Delights
African American Delights
Australian Delights
Austrian Delights

Brazilian Delights
Canadian Delights
Chilean Delights
Chinese Delights
Czechoslovakian Delights
English Delights
Ethiopian Delights
Fijian Delights
French Delights
German Delights
Greek Delights
Hungarian Delights
Icelandic Delights
Indian Delights
Irish Delights
Italian Delights
Korean Delights
Mexican Delights
Native American Delights
Polish Delights
Russian Delights
Scottish Delights
Slovenian Delights
Swedish Delights
Thai Delights
The Netherlands Delights
Yugoslavian Delights
Zambian Delights

REGIONAL DELIGHTS

Glacier National Park Delights
Northwest Regional Delights
Oregon Coast Delights
Schweitzer Mountain Delights
Southwest Regional Delights
Tropical Delights
Washington Wine Country Delights
Wine Delights of Walla Walla Wineries
Yellowstone National Park Delights

SEASONAL DELIGHTS

Autumn Harvest Delights
Spring Harvest Delights
Summer Harvest Delights
Winter Harvest Delights

SPECIAL EVENTS DELIGHTS

Birthday Delights
Coffee Klatch Delights
Super Bowl Delights
Tea Time Delights

STATE DELIGHTS

Alaska Delights
Arizona Delights
Georgia Delights
Hawaii Delights
Idaho Delights
Illinois Delights
Iowa Delights
Louisiana Delights
Minnesota Delights
Montana Delights
North Dakota Delights
Oregon Delights
South Dakota Delights
Texas Delights
Washington Delights

U.S. TERRITORIES DELIGHTS

Cruzan Delights
U.S. Virgin Island Delights

MISCELLANEOUS COOKBOOKS

Getaway Studio Cookbook
The Soup Doctor's Cookbook

BILINGUAL DELIGHTS SERIES

Apple Delights, English-French Edition
Apple Delights, English-Russian Edition
Apple Delights, English-Spanish Edition

Huckleberry Delights, English-French Edition
Huckleberry Delights, English-Russian Edition
Huckleberry Delights, English-Spanish Edition

CATHOLIC DELIGHTS SERIES

Apple Delights Catholic
Coffee Delights Catholic
Easter Delights Catholic
Huckleberry Delights Catholic
Tea Delights Catholic

CATHOLIC BILINGUAL DELIGHTS SERIES

Apple Delights Catholic, English-French Edition
Apple Delights Catholic, English-Russian Edition
Apple Delights Catholic, English-Spanish Edition
Huckleberry Delights Catholic, English-Spanish Edition

CHRISTIAN DELIGHTS SERIES

Apple Delights Christian
Coffee Delights Christian
Easter Delights Christian
Huckleberry Delights Christian
Tea Delights Christian

CHRISTIAN BILINGUAL DELIGHTS SERIES

Apple Delights Christian, English-French Edition
Apple Delights Christian, English-Russian Edition
Apple Delights Christian, English-Spanish Edition
Huckleberry Delights Christian, English-Spanish Edition

FUNDRAISING COOKBOOKS

Ask about our fundraising cookbooks to help raise funds for your organization.

The above books are also available in bilingual versions. Please contact Whispering Pine Press International, Inc., for details.

**Please note that some books are future books and are currently in production. Please contact us for availability date. Prices are subject to change without notice.*

The above list of books is not all-inclusive. For a complete list please visit our website or contact us at:

Whispering Pine Press International, Inc
Your Northwest Book Publishing Company
P.O. Box 214
Spokane Valley, WA 99037-0214 USA
Phone: (509) 928-8700 | Fax: (509) 922-9949
Email: sales@WhisperingPinePress.com
Publisher Websites: www.WhisperingPinePress.com
www.WhisperingPinePressBookstore.com
Blog: www.WhisperingPinePressBlog.com

Onion Delights

A Collection of Onion Recipes
Cookbook Delights Series-Book 8

Karen Jean Matsko Hood

Published by:

Whispering Pine Press International, Inc.
Your Northwest Book Publishing Company
P.O. Box 214
Spokane Valley, WA 99037-0214 USA
Phone: (509) 928-8700 | Fax: (509) 922-9949
Email: sales@WhisperingPinePress.com
Websites: www.WhisperingPinePress.com
www.WhisperingPinePressBookStore.com
Blog: www.WhisperingPinePressBlog.com
SAN 253-200X
Printed in the U.S.A.

Published by Whispering Pine Press International, Inc.
P.O. Box 214
Spokane Valley, Washington 99037-0214 USA

For sales outside the United States, please contact the Whispering Pine Press International, Inc., International Sales Department.

Manufactured in the United States of America. This paper is acid-free and 100% chlorine free.

Book and Cover Design by Artistic Design Service, Inc.
P. O. Box 1792
Spokane Valley, WA 99037-1792 USA
www.ArtisticDesignService.com

Library of Congress Number (LCCN): 2014901412

Hood, Karen Jean Matsko
Title: Onion Delights Cookbook: A Collection of Onion Recipes: Cookbook Delights Series-Book 8

p. cm.

ISBN: 978-1-59808-664-5 case bound
ISBN: 978-1-59808-662-1 perfect bound
ISBN: 978-1-59649-995-9 spiral bound
ISBN: 978-1-59649-994-2 comb bound
ISBN: 978-1-59649-996-6 E-PDF
ISBN: 978-1-59210-426-0 E-PUB
ISBN: 978-1-59434-864-8 E-PRC

First Edition: January 2014
1. Cookery *(Onion Delights Cookbook: A Collection of Onion Recipes: Cookbook Delights Series-Book 8)* 1. Title

Onion Delights Cookbook

A Collection of Onion Recipes
Cookbook Delights Series-Book 8

Gift Inscription

To: ______________________________

From: ______________________________

Date: ______________________________

Special Message: ______________________________

____

____

____

____

____

____

____

____

It is always nice to receive a personal note to create a special memory.

www.OnionDelightsCookbook.com
www.WhisperingPinePress.com
www.WhisperingPinePressBookstore.com

Dedications

To my husband and best friend, Jim.

To our seventeen children: Gabriel, Brianne Kristina and her husband Moulik Kothari, Marissa Kimberly, Janelle Karina and her husband Paul Turcotte, Mikayla Karlene, Kyler James, Kelsey Katrina, Corbin Joel, Caleb Jerome, Keisha Kalani Hiwot, Devontay Joshua, Kianna Karielle Selam, Rosy Kiara, Mercedes Katherine, Jasmine Khalia Wengel, Cheyenne Krystal, and Annalise Kaylee Marie.

To our grandchild Nola Paige, and our future grandchildren.

To our foster grandchildren: Courtney, Lorenzo and Leah.

To my brother, Stephen, and his wife, Karen.

To my husband's ten siblings: Gary, Colleen, John, Dan, Mary, Ray, Ann, Teresa, Barbara, Agnes, and their families.

In loving memory of my mom, who passed away in 2007; my dad, who passed away in 1976; and my sister, Sandy, who passed away due to multiple sclerosis in 1999.

To Sandy's three sons: Monte, Bradley, and Derek. To Monte's wife, Sarah, and their children: Liam, Alice, Charlie, and Samuel and their foster children. To Bradley's wife, Shawnda, and their children: Anton, Isaac, and Isabel.

To our foster children past and present: Krystal, Sara, Rebecca, Janice, Devontay Joshua, Mercedes Katherine, Zha'Nell, Makia, Onna, Cheyenne Krystal, Onna Marie, Nevaeh, and Zada, our future foster children, and all foster children everywhere.

To the Court Appointed Special Advocate (CASA) Volunteer Program in the judicial system which benefits abused and neglected children.

To the Literacy Campaign dedicated to promoting literacy throughout the world.

Acknowledgements

The author would like to acknowledge all those individuals who helped me during my time in writing this book. Appreciation is extended for all their support and effort they put into this project.

Deep gratitude and profound thanks are owed to my husband, Jim, for giving freely of his time and encouragement during this project.

Thanks are owed to my children Gabriel, Brianne Kristina and her husband Moulik Kothari, Marissa Kimberly, Janelle Karina and her husband Paul Turcotte, Mikayla Karlene, Kyler James, Kelsey Katrina, Corbin Joel, Caleb Jerome, Keisha Kalani Hiwot, Devontay Joshua, Kianna Karielle Selam, Rosy Kiara, Mercedes Katherine, Jasmine Khalia Wengel, Cheyenne Krystal, and Annalise Kaylee Marie. All of these persons inspire my writing.

Thanks are due to Teresa L. Allen and Sharron Thompson for their assistance in typing this manuscript for publication. Thanks go to Artistic Design Service, Inc. for their assistance in formatting and providing a graphic design of this manuscript for publication. This project could not have been completed without them.

Many thanks are due to members of my family, all of whom were very supportive during the time it took to complete this project. Their patience and support are greatly appreciated.

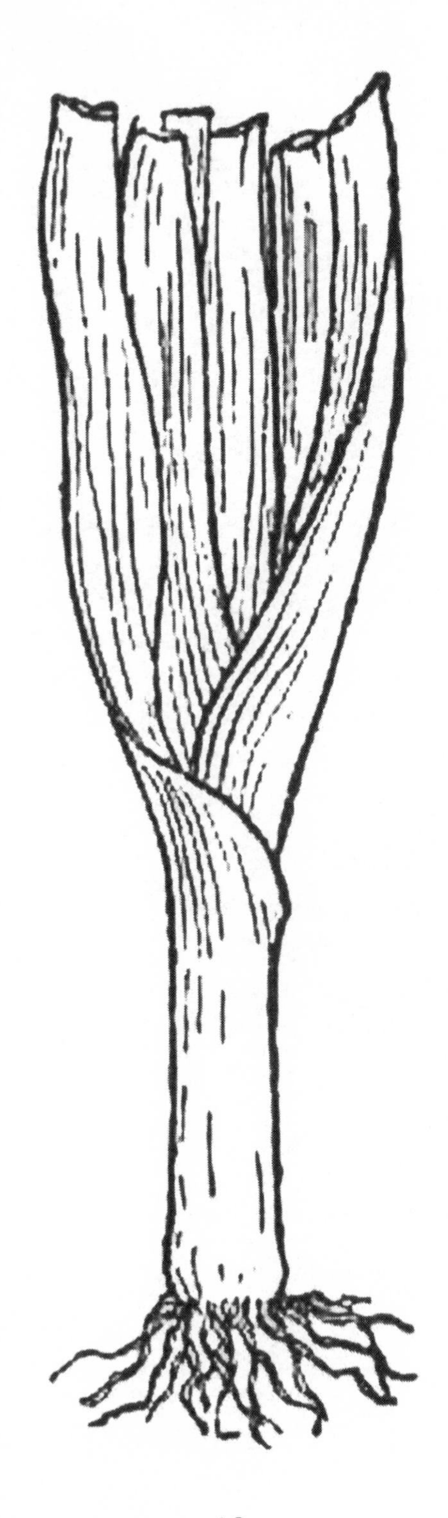

Onion Delights Cookbook

Table of Contents

Onion Delights Cookbook

A Collection of Onion Recipes
Cookbook Delights Series-Book 8

Introduction

Living in the heart of Washington brings great appreciation for sweet Walla Walla onions. All varieties of the onion are distinct in shape, size, color, and flavor, and all have their own appeal. The most common type of onion commercially produced is the yellow onion.

Onions add texture and a delicious flavor to almost any dish you prepare. You may be surprised to know that onions can even be used in desserts and other unlikely dishes. From the potent to the sweet varieties, onions take their place as one of the most common vegetables in the average consumer's refrigerator.

Since onions have been cultivated from as early as 2000 B.C. in ancient Egypt, they have an interesting history of facts and folklore. Some of this folklore is included in this book. As a poet, I found it enjoyable to color this cookbook with poetry so that readers could savor the metaphorical richness of the onion as well as its literal flavor. Also included in this *Onion Delights Cookbook* are some articles on history, cultivation, and botanical information, along with some interesting quotes and tidbits.

This cookbook is organized in convenient alphabetical sections to assist you in finding recipes related to the type of cooking you need: appetizers and dips; beverages; breads and rolls; breakfasts; cakes; candies; cookies; desserts; dressings, sauces, and condiments; jams, jellies, and syrups; main dishes; pies; preserving; salads; side dishes; soups; and wines and spirits.

Following is a collection of recipes gathered and modified to bring you *Onion Delights Cookbook: A Collection of Onion Recipes, Cookbook Delights Series* by Karen Jean Matsko Hood.

Onion
Botanical Classification

Onion Botanical Classification

The onion comes from *Liliaceae* (the lily family), which is the same genus (*Allium*) as chives (*A. schoenoprasum*), leek (*A. porrum*), garlic (*A. sativum*), and shallots (*A. ascalonium*). All of these plants are rich in sugar and pungent oil, which is the source of the strong flavor in plants of this family. Onions also produce long, green shoots above the surface which are also eaten. The onion (*A. cepa*) is a biennial crop grown worldwide in an astounding number of varieties.

Onions come in many varieties, each with its own particular strength and flavor. Stronger flavored onions tend to be red or purple in color, while yellow onions tend to be a bit milder. White onions are generally the mildest, many possessing an almost sweet flavor. Pearl onions are white, small onions often used in pickling. Bermuda onions tend to have an elusive, subtle flavor.

The shallot (purportedly introduced in Europe by the Crusaders) is a perennial plant with small clusters of bulbs that closely resemble onions. Shallots and leeks (a biennial plant featuring one small bulb), are commonly used in salads, soups, and stews.

Scallion is the term for any edible *Allium* with a smaller bulb. The Welsh onion (*A. fistulosum*) is similar to the leek, and popular in Asia. The chive grows wild in Greece and Italy. Its leaves are used as a flavorful herb.

Onion Cultivation and Gardening

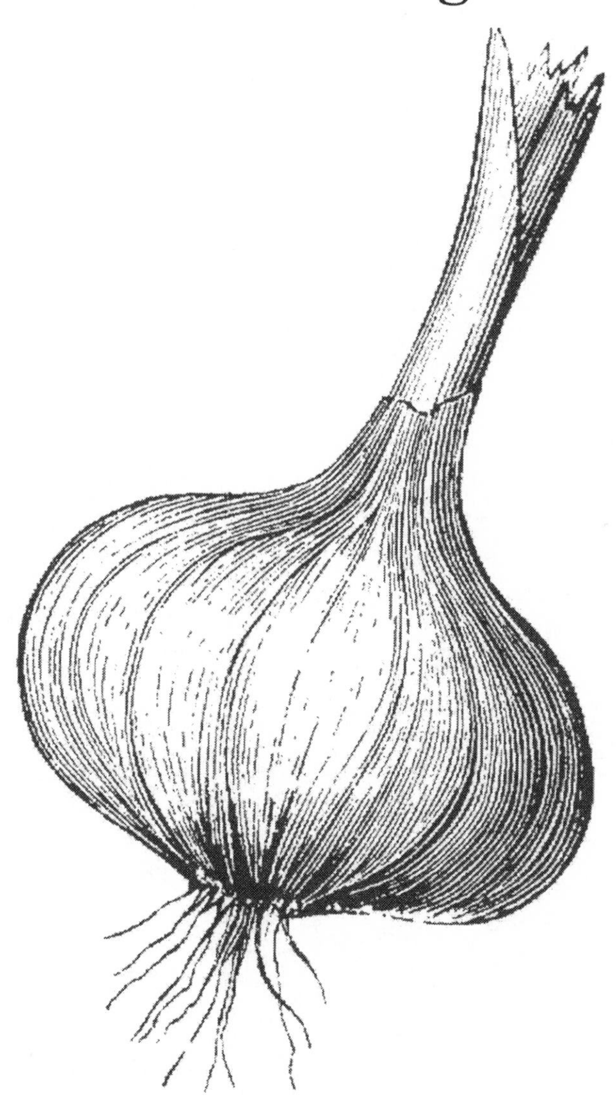

Onion Cultivation and Gardening

The onion is a vegetable that is grown successfully throughout most of North America. Onions may be grown from sets, transplants, or seeds. Onions only begin bulb formation when the length of the day is of the correct duration, and not all onions require the same day-lengths in order to initiate bulbing.

Generally speaking, most common onion varieties are either long-day (northern latitudes) or short-day (southern latitudes). Because of this, onions must be grown in the correct latitude in order to successfully flourish.

Low humidity and high temperatures are beneficial during the bulbing and curing processes. This is because onions have only shallow roots and thus are easily choked by weeds. Shallow hoeing and careful cultivation are of extreme importance, especially when onion plants are small.

Onions From Sets

The simplest method for home gardeners is to grow green onions from sets. They establish themselves quickly and soon become robust. Onion sets can produce either green onions or dry onion bulb. For best results producing bulbs, however, read the following section.

Onions From Transplants

In order to grow larger, more attractive onions suitable for slicing, one must grow from transplants. Transplants can be purchased in bunches from garden stores and nursery catalogs.

Recommended Varieties

There are a wide variety of sets available to the home gardener. However, simply buying sets from a local store will usually provide only limited varieties of sets, merely sold by their color and not their variety name.

It is advisable to purchase your sets early, before they have begun to grow in the salesrooms. Be sure to store your sets in a cool, dark place if you won't be planting right away. Larger, white sets are best used for growing green onions, and smaller sets are best for growing bulbs. As a general rule, elongated sets will mature into round onions, while round sets mature into flat onions.

Garden centers generally offer the following sets:

Yellow Sweet Spanish
White Sweet Spanish
Yellow Bermuda
White Bermuda

Catalog shoppers may choose from a slightly wider variety selection, including:

Texas Grano
Vidalia Sweet
Red Hamburger
Walla Walla Sweet
Texas 1015Y Supersweet

When to Plant

Onions should be planted as soon as your garden is ready to till in the spring, normally by late March or early April. You should have adequate soil moisture, good fertility, and cool temperatures also aid in onion development.

Spacing and Depth

To grow green onions, plant your larger sets 1½ inches deep and close enough to be touching (green onions should be harvested before overcrowding sets in). To grow dry onions, plant your smaller sets 1 inch deep, with 2 to 4 inches between sets. Allow 14 to 18 inches between rows. If sets are set 2 inches apart, be sure to harvest every other plant as a green onion so development of the remaining sets isn't hampered by neighboring plants.

Care

Keep onions free from weeds by shallow cultivation and hoeing. If you would like to develop nice, long stems on your green onions, make small "hills" around the onions by pulling loose soil toward them. Grass and weeds compete with onion plants for moisture and nutrients. Remove all weeds and grass by repeated shallow hoeing and cultivation. You may need to use fertilizer.

Harvesting

You may harvest green onions anytime after their tops measure at least 6 inches tall. The larger the green onion, the stronger it will taste. If your green onions become so strong as to be unfit for eating raw, they may still be used for cooking. Pull any plants that have formed flower stalks and use them immediately. It is best to harvest late in July or early in August, after most of the plant tops have begun to droop. You should allow this to occur naturally, and not force the tops to droop.

Pull your mature onions early in the day and let the bulbs air dry until later in the day. In order to completely dry and cure your onion bulbs, you will need to hang them up to dry for a good 2 to 3 weeks in place with good air circulation. Do not remove the dry, outer layer of the onions, as this will serve to keep them from spoiling. After they have dried, be sure to store the onions in a cool, dry place. They should remain good until winter, but check often for signs of softening or rot.

Onion Facts

Onion Facts

The word "onion" comes from the Latin word *unio* meaning "single" or "one," because the onion plant produces a single bulb, unlike its cousin, the garlic, that produces many small bulbs. The name also describes the many separate, concentrically arranged layers of the onion.

Onions have been cultivated and eaten since the dawn of humankind. They were mentioned in first dynasty of ancient Egypt, circa 3200 B.C., and appeared in paintings, documents, and inscriptions from that time on. Onions have been depicted in paintings heaped onto banquet tables. Onions were a staple food of the poor Egyptians, but were also revered as a spiritual symbol.

The concentric layers of onion bulbs were representative of eternal life and therefore were often used as funeral offerings and as part of sacrifices. When King Ramses IV died, small onions were placed on his eyes, which were later discovered by archeologists.

When onions are sliced, their cells break open and release certain enzymes and amino acids that combine to form sulphenic acids, which dissipate into the air. This is why chopping onions makes your eyes water. One way to prevent this from happening is to cut the onions under running water or submerged in water. Another remedy often used by Italians is to hold a small piece of bread against the roof of your mouth with your tongue, which seems to lesson irritation.

The onion was considered as valuable as gold in the Middle Ages.

Paintings of onions appear on the inner walls of the pyramids and in the tombs of both the Old Kingdom and the New Kingdom

School biology laboratories often use onions because they have large cells, easily visible even using the most basic of microscopes.

Onion Folklore

Onion Folklore

The strong odor of onions seemed mysterious to ancient peoples. There is an old legend explaining that when Satan was evicted from heaven, garlic sprouted where his left foot landed, and onions grew where his right foot landed.

When Eastern Europe was afflicted by plagues, many attributed the disease to evil spirits, using onions and garlic to ward them off. Onions and garlic have been strung from doorways, windows, and even around people's necks as a vampire repellent.

Some cultures believed onions and garlic increased libido and sexual stamina. Even today, grooms in certain cultures will wear a clove of garlic on their lapels to assure a good wedding night.

In India, onions were once used as a diuretic. They were supposed to be good for the heart, eyes, and joints. In the colonial United States, a bit of wild onion was thought to cure measles.

In ancient China, onions were supposed to calm the liver, moisten intestines, and promote healthy lungs. They were also prescribed for constipation, and to heal wounds.

In ancient Greece, athletes ate onions to "lighten the balance of the blood."

Onion-domed towers were favored in Russia and Eastern Europe because it was believed that they would allow the building to last forever.

Onions have been regarded as a cure for baldness. Bald men were supposed to rub a piece of onion over their heads. The juice of the onion supposedly caused their hair to grow back thicker than ever. Nothing is mentioned about how it would smell!

Onions have a variety of medicinal effects. Early American settlers used wild onions to treat colds, coughs, and asthma, and to repel insects. In Chinese medicine, onions have been used to treat angina, coughs, bacterial infections, and breathing problems.

Onion Delights Cookbook
A Collection of Onion Recipes
Cookbook Delights Series-Book 8

Onion History

Onion History

Most researchers agree that the onion has been cultivated for 5,000 years or more. Since onions grew wild in various regions, they were probably consumed for thousands of years and domesticated simultaneously all over the world. Onions may be one of the earliest cultivated crops because they were less perishable than other foods of the time, transportable, easy to grow, and could be grown in a variety of soils and climates. In addition, the onion was useful for sustaining human life. Onions prevented thirst and could be dried and preserved for later consumption when food might be scarce.

Onions are mentioned to have been eaten by the Israelites in the Bible. In Numbers 11:5, the children of Israel lament the meager desert diet enforced by the Exodus: "We remember the fish, which we did eat in Egypt freely, the cucumbers and the melons and the leeks and the onions and the garlic."

The first Pilgrims brought onions with them on the *Mayflower*. However, they found that strains of wild onions already grew throughout North America. Native Americans used wild onions in a variety of ways, eating them raw or cooked, as a seasoning or as a vegetable. Such onions were also used in syrups, as poultices, as an ingredient in dyes, and even as toys. According to diaries of colonists, bulb onions were planted as soon as the Pilgrim fathers could clear the land in 1648.

Until the twentieth century, onions were relegated as food for the poor. The Code of Hammurabi, the ancient law of Mesopotamia, provided the needy with a monthly ration of bread and onions, the foundation of the peasant diet. In addition to serving as a food for both the poor and the wealthy, onions were prescribed to alleviate headaches, snakebites, and hair loss. They were also used as rent payments and wedding gifts.

The bustling city of Chicago was named for a variety of onion the Native Americans called Chicago.

Onion
Nutrition and Health

Onion Nutrition and Health

All members of the onion family offer some protection against heart disease. Research suggests that oils in onions help to lower LDL in the blood stream while increasing HDL levels. Mature, dry onions are also a good source of fiber. Only scallions and green onions contain vitamin A.

If you're counting calories, you might want to take advantage of the low calorie content of sweet raw onions. With ½ cup of chopped raw onions, you'll tally up a mere 30 calories. If you cook those same onions, you are up to only 46 calories.

On the protein scene, ½ cup of cooked onions touts nearly 1½ grams, while the raw have less than 1 gram. The folic acid content offers a surprising 15.8 micrograms for the cooked, and 15.2 micrograms for raw.

Both raw and cooked onions have trace amounts of B vitamins, iron, and zinc, but stand out with potassium, magnesium, and calcium. While potassium registers 174.3 milligrams for ½ cup cooked onions, raw onions come in at 125.6 milligrams. Raw and cooked onions deliver 5.5 milligrams and 5.1 milligrams of vitamin C, respectively. Raw scallions pack a powerful punch of vitamin A with 193 IU for ½ cup, with their tops. Folic acid registers 32.0 micrograms, and vitamin C at 9.4 milligrams. Onions are low in sodium and contain no fat.

And don't forget the powerful antioxidants, including quercetin, delivered by onions. Some nutritionists think quercetin is an anti-cancer agent.

Some of the onions beneficial properties are seen after long-term usage. Onion may be a useful herb for the prevention of cardiovascular disease, especially since they diminish the risk of blood clots. Onion also protects against stomach and other cancers, as well as protecting against certain infections. Onion can improve lung function, especially in asthmatics. The more pungent varieties of onion appear to possess the greatest concentration of health-promoting phytochemicals.

Onion Delights Cookbook
A Collection of Onion Recipes
Cookbook Delights Series-Book 8

Poetry

A Collection of Poetry with Onion Themes

Table of Contents

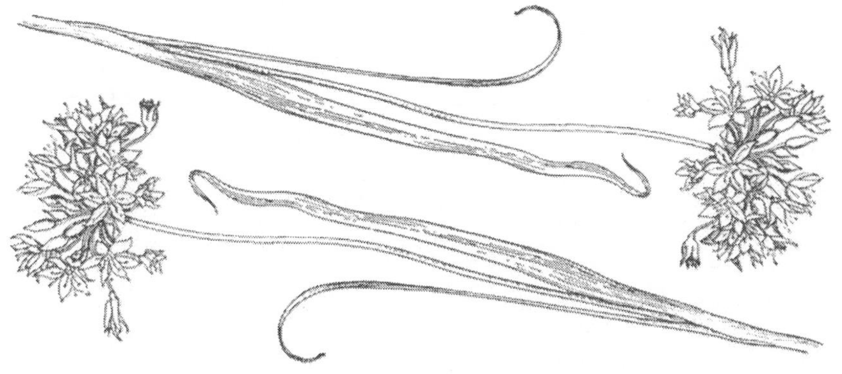

Motherly Gardening

My mother
Taught me
To garden
To dig with bare hands
In clay and
Loam,
And crawl with
Montana angleworms,
That shine in dim
Rays that reflect
From Big
Sky.
My mind
Wanders
Through the
muck,
Reddish heavy,
Muddy ooze.
Intrigued with
Life
And worms,
Those bugs
Slink through
The gumbo,
Slip
in its
Heaviness.
Great Falls' wind
Reminds
Me to
Plant those
Seeds
Before Chinook
Winds come
To make
More mud.
Wise old mom
Knew that
Earthen mire
Grounded me
In ways
Earthworms
Inch and
Always understand.

Karen Jean Matsko Hood ©2014
Published in *Onion Delights Cookbook*, 2014
By Whispering Pine Press International, Inc., 2014

Moonlit Sun

How long will be my life?
I asked under the sunlit moon.
It seems I want to trade
My days of the magical
Worker bee with the giant
Sea turtle to bask in the
Hushful moonlit sun.

Karen Jean Matsko Hood ©2014
Published in *Onion Delights Cookbook*, 2014
By Whispering Pine Press International, Inc., 2014

Wrinkled Gardener

The furrowed face
Upon the man
Gardening with his wrinkles
As he plowed the land.

I watched this wise old soul
Sow his seeds by hand,
Then studied the liver spots
Upon his freckled forearms.

His back was curved and matched the face.
Countenance of the man haggard and worn,
Full of wisdom of years gone by.
Understanding as he stroked the ground.

He seemed to whisper to the soil,
To know the wind,
To listen to every reverberation
Expressed by the soul of the earth.

I wish I knew what was said,
What Mother Earth told this gentleman,
Instead, I have a novel unanimity
Of the detail in the gardener's face print.

Karen Jean Matsko Hood©2014
Published in *Onion Delights Cookbook*, 2014
By Whispering Pine Press International, Inc., 2014

Onions on the Grill

Tears drip down her cheeks
as she holds the steel blade
and perfects each slice.

Down the road at Hudson's,
a man stands behind a grill,
the old-fashioned variety.

There he quickly slices onions
as fast as he can to bring
back nostalgia to those who
crave the old days.

That bygone period of time.

Karen Jean Matsko Hood ©2014
Published in *Onion Delights Cookbook*, 2014
By Whispering Pine Press International, Inc., 2014

Onion Delights

Layers upon layers,
circle upon circle
coil to the center
of the onion delight.

White, yellow, red, purple,
sweet, hot. All a part
of onion delights.

Warm fragrance permeates the air
as onions sauté on the stove.
Savory flavor bakes in homemade bread.

Published in *Onion Delights Cookbook*, 2014
By Whispering Pine Press International, Inc., 2014

Onion Layers

She was like the onion
A collection of layers
stratified one upon the other.

We can peel away the skin
to find the protection of each layer.

Callous Colors

Fragile, old, yet vigorous
Marie walks outside to pick the iris.
Gaudy headscarf adorns her bald head.

Respect she shows to each fine iris that
struggles with scarred petals in the weather.
Now they emote sturdy resistance.

Cancer has taken over Marie's bones,
while the hailstorm ravages
fields of iris blossoms as they stand proud.

This sixty-year-old lady is far too
young to succumb to nature;
iris blossoms, as gallant flags,
reassure her.

Marie glances as the
crystal twinkles,
purple iris in its prism.

Butterflies stop to
kiss the harmony,
gentle in the breeze.

Slowly the sun
fades, to bring
final rest for the
kind zephyr.

Published in *Onion Delights Cookbook*, 2014
By Whispering Pine Press International, Inc., 2014

Mask of Layers

Take off your mask, dear love.
Your shiny, painted, beautiful mask.
Tiny flaws and cracks
Hiding behind lacquered layers
Revealing mundane colors
Waiting to come alive.
Peel off the arrogance and
Throw it on the glass panes
Windowsill. Leave it there
To rest so I can see
Your fine sullen eyes. The
Windows to your soul.
Asleep in two caves.

Published in *Onion Delights Cookbook*, 2014
By Whispering Pine Press International, Inc., 2014

See the Glory

I want to share the goodness
Of this wonderful world:
Truth, justice, love,
Fragrant roses, daffodils and lilacs,
Velvet petals and soothing blades of grass.
Fall onto your back
At peace. Look up
At the clouds.
See the glory!

Published in *Onion Delights Cookbook*, 2014
By Whispering Pine Press International, Inc., 2014

Onion Types

Onion Types

There are over 600 species of onions distributed all over Europe, North America, Northern Africa, and Asia. The plants can be used as ornamentals, vegetables, spices, or as medicine.

Food historians are not certain about the precise origin of the onion. Although some types of onions have been given names like Egyptian onions or Welsh onions, there is little evidence to suggest they actually grew in those countries. For example, the Welsh onion (*Allium fistulosum*), is considered quite primitive because it has never developed a bulb but more resembles a scallion with a slightly thickened stem. The Welsh did not cultivate them on a large scale, and they were not brought into the country until 1629.

Columbus introduced European varieties to the New World. They were much stronger in their flavor than the native varieties, and the Native Americans were quick to adopt these new onions into their diet.

Onions are available in four colors or shades of colors: yellow, red, green, and white. Most onions grown in the United States are yellow onions, and only about 15 percent of crops grown include red, white, and green onions.

Yellow onions are great; all-purpose onions that can be used in just about any recipe. Yellow onions turn color when cooked, from transparent to dark brown and lend French onion soup its tangy flavor. Red onions are fairly strong, have great color, and are a good choice for salads or in grilling. White onions tend to be the sweetest, and when sautéed, take on a caramel color and sweet flavor. They are often used in Mexican cuisine, while green onions are mostly used fresh in salads, or as garnishes to a dish.

Today most of the onions eaten in North America are storage onions. Most of them are grown in western Idaho and eastern Oregon. In fact, onions are grown for commercial purposes in 26 states, with California, Texas, New York, Michigan, and Colorado joining Idaho and Oregon as the major suppliers.

Onion Delights Cookbook
A Collection of Onion Recipes
Cookbook Delights Series-Book 8

RECIPES

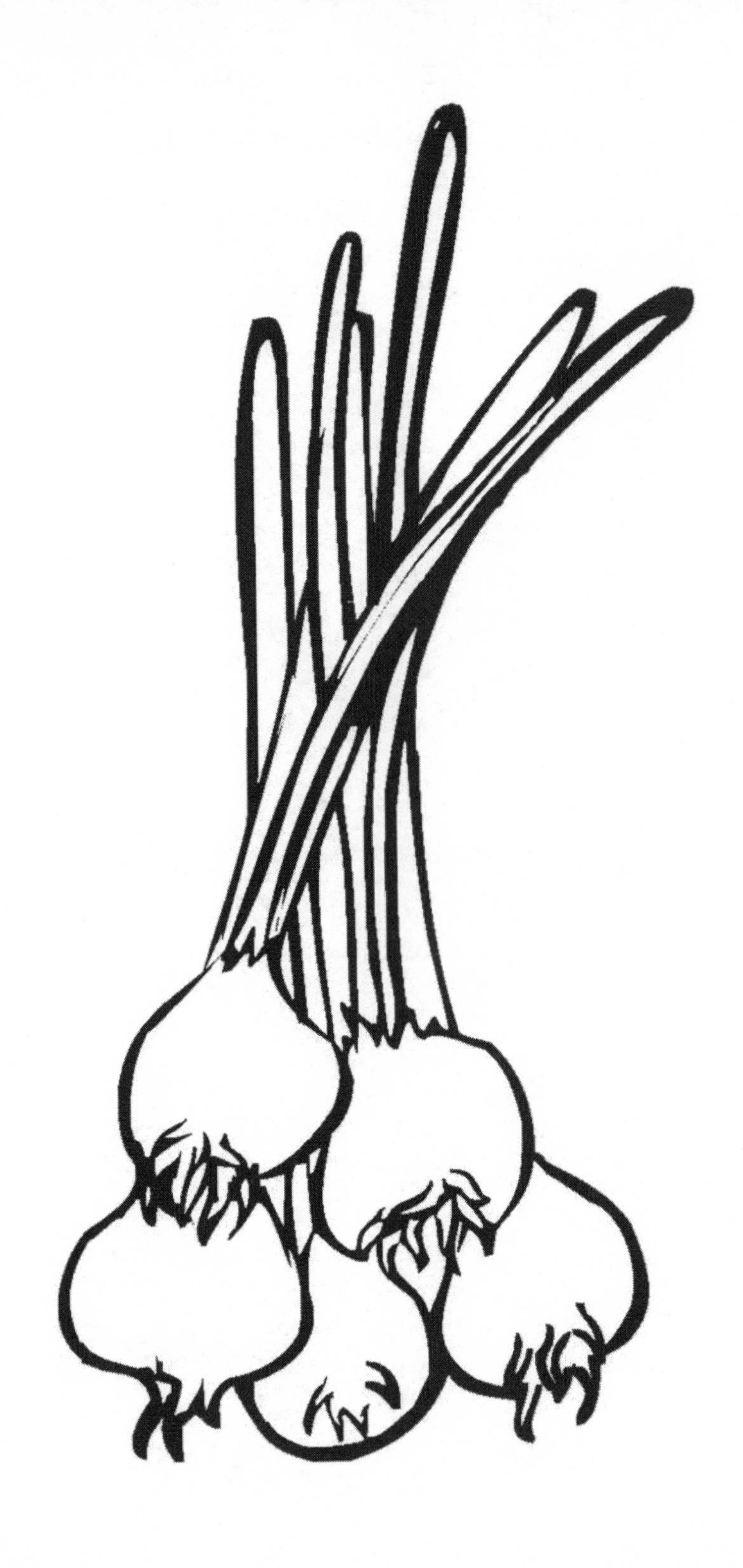

Appetizers and Dips

Table of Contents

Alaskan King Crab Cocktail

Our family loves crab, and this recipe makes a delicious appetizer for special occasions.

Ingredients for crab cocktail:

1½ c. red and yellow peppers, finely chopped
½ c. sweet onion, chopped
1½ c. celery, finely chopped
3 c. Alaskan king crab meat
lettuce or spinach leaves

Ingredients for cocktail sauce:

1 c. ketchup
2 Tbs. horseradish
2 tsp. hot sauce
1 tsp. white pepper
1 tsp. black pepper
1 tsp. salt
½ tsp. garlic powder
1 tsp. onion powder

Directions for crab cocktail:

1. To assemble the crab cocktail, line serving dish with lettuce or spinach leaves.
2. In large bowl, combine red and yellow peppers, sweet onion, and celery.
3. Stir crabmeat in gently, to avoid breaking up the large lumps of crabmeat.
4. Heap the crabmeat mixture onto the greens; refrigerate and chill.
5. When ready to serve, remove from refrigerator, and spoon the chilled cocktail sauce over the salad.

Directions for cocktail sauce:

1. In small bowl, combine ketchup, horseradish, and hot sauce; blend well.
2. Add white and black pepper, salt, garlic powder, and onion powder; blend well.
3. Adjust seasonings to taste; chill at least 1 hour.

Beer Battered Onion Rings

These onion rings are very savory and easy to make. Try them while watching the big game!

Ingredients:

1 c. flour, plus extra for dusting
1 c. beer
2 sweet onions, peeled, cut crosswise ⅓-inch thick
canola oil, for deep-frying
salt, to taste

Directions:

1. Place 1 cup flour into a bowl; make a well in the center.
2. Pour beer into the well; whisk until the mixture is combined.
3. Strain batter through a sieve into a clean bowl and let rest, covered, for 1 hour.
4. Separate onion slices into rings and dust rings with additional flour, shaking off excess.
5. Dip and coat in batter just enough rings at a time that will fit in the pan of oil.
6. Preheat 2 inches of oil to 370 degrees F. Fry onion rings in batches until they are golden.
7. Transfer with slotted spoon to paper towels to drain; sprinkle with salt, to taste.

Blooming Onions and Dipping Sauce

These are worth the time they take to make, and the sauce is also very good. I have included directions to cut the onions by hand, but if you prefer, you can use a blooming onion device to save you some time.

Ingredients for blooming onion sauce:

1 c. mayonnaise
2 Tbs. ketchup
4 Tbs. cream style horseradish sauce
⅔ tsp. paprika
¼ tsp. oregano, dried
⅔ tsp. cayenne pepper
½ tsp. salt
dash ground black pepper

Ingredients for blooming onions:

2 eggs
2 c. milk
2 c. flour
1½ tsp. salt
3 tsp. cayenne pepper
2 tsp. paprika
1 tsp. black pepper, ground
⅔ tsp. oregano, dried
¼ tsp. thyme, dried
¼ tsp. cumin, dried
2 lg. sweet onions
canola or peanut oil, for frying

Directions for sauce:

1. In medium bowl, combine mayonnaise, ketchup, horseradish, paprika, and oregano; blend well.
2. Add cayenne, salt and black pepper to taste; mix well.
3. Cover and place in refrigerator until ready to serve.

Directions for onions:

1. In medium bowl, beat eggs and add milk.

2. In separate bowl, combine flour, salt, cayenne pepper, paprika, ground black pepper, oregano, thyme and cumin; mix well.
3. Slice 1 inch off top of onion; just above the roots of the bottom of onion, cut the papery skin layers all the way around and remove.
4. Use a 3 to 4-inch length, thin bladed knife, to cut a 1-inch diameter core out of the middle of onion.
5. Use a very sharp, larger knife to slice onion several times down the center to create petals; by first slicing through center of onion to ¾ of the way down. Do not cut down to bottom of onion.
6. Turn onion half way around and slice across the first cut.
7. Keep slicing sections of the onion in half starting from the center to the outside, very carefully, as you hold the onion firmly around outside, until onion has been cut into 16 wedges.
8. The last 8 slices will be difficult, as those sections are quite small in width; go slowly and be careful.
9. Gently spread petals of onion apart.
10. To help keep them separate, plunge onion into boiling water for 1 minute, then into cold water.
11. Dip onion into milk mixture and coat it liberally with flour mixture.
12. Again, separate petals and sprinkle dry coating between them.
13. Once the onion is well coated, dip it back into wet mixture and into dry coating again.
14. This double dipping ensures you have a well coated onion since some of the coating will wash off when placed in the frying oil.
15. Heat oil in deep fryer or deep pot to 350 degrees F.
16. Be certain that you use enough oil to completely cover onion when it fries, using a deep enough vessel to allow for bubbling oil not to spill over sides.
17. Fry onion right side up in oil for 10 minutes, or until it turns brown; occasionally dunking onion under oil to be sure it is cooking and browning on top.
18. When onion has browned, remove from oil and let drain on rack or paper towels.
19. Open onion wider from center so you can put small dish of dipping sauce in center or place dish on the side. Serve while warm.

Creamy Onion Dip

This is a delicious onion dip that will be a hit at your next party.

Ingredients:

2 c. onions, finely chopped
1 Tbs. olive oil
1 tsp. paprika
1 c. sour cream
salt and pepper, to taste

Directions:

1. In large skillet, heat oil.
2. Add onions; sauté over medium heat for 3 minutes, or until just tender; stir in paprika.
3. Remove from heat.
4. In medium bowl, combine onion mixture and sour cream.
5. Add salt and pepper to taste; stir well to blend.
6. Cover and refrigerate until ready to serve.

Dijon and Onion Dip on Rounds

Dijon mustard and Parmesan cheese make this green onion dip on bread rounds a real treat. Make a large batch, as it will go fast.

Ingredients:

1 c. mayonnaise
½ c. fresh Parmesan cheese, grated
2 Tbs. Dijon mustard
2 green onions, chopped
1 French bread baguette, sliced diagonally (40 pieces)
ripe olives, sliced

Directions:

1. In small bowl, combine mayonnaise, cheese, mustard, and onions until well blended.
2. Spread approximately 2 tablespoons mixture on each bread slice.
3. Place slices with cheese side up on a baking sheet.
4. Garnish each with a few ripe olive slices just before broiling.
5. Broil until lightly browned.
6. Serve while hot.

Hungarian Cheese Spread

This is a delicious cheese spread. Anchovy lovers will especially enjoy it.

Ingredients:

1 c. cream cheese, softened
6 Tbs. sour cream
1 Tbs. prepared mustard
2 tsp. Hungarian paprika
3 lg. green onions, finely chopped
1 tsp. anchovy paste

Directions:

1. In large bowl, combine cream cheese, sour cream, mustard, and paprika; blend well with fork.
2. Fold in onions and anchovy, stirring lightly.
3. Serve as a spread on thinly sliced pumpernickel bread.
4. Note: Use can also use as a dip for veggies by adding more sour cream until mixture reaches dipping consistency.

Onion Rings West Texas Style

These tangy Texan onion rings are sure to make your taste buds sing!

Ingredients:

2 lg. sweet onions, about 1 lb. each
1½ c. milk or buttermilk
1½ c. flour, divided
2 Tbs. adobo sauce
1½ c. yellow cornmeal
1 Tbs. ground cumin
1½ tsp. salt, plus more for seasoning
canola oil, for frying

Directions:

1. Cut sweet onions horizontally into ½-inch thick slices.
2. Separate into rings.
3. In large mixing bowl, whisk milk, ½ cup of the flour, and adobo sauce until smooth; add onion rings and toss to moisten.
4. In large bowl, combine remaining 1 cup flour with the cornmeal, cumin, and salt.
5. Working in batches, remove onions from milk mixture; dredge onions in cornmeal mix, shaking off excess.
6. Transfer to baking sheet, until enough to cover surface of oil in skillet.
7. Repeat steps 4 and 5 for each batch.
8. Fry each batch of onion rings in skillet of oil preheated to 350 degrees F. until golden brown.
9. Using tongs, transfer to paper towels to drain.
10. Season with salt and serve immediately.

Buttermilk Onion Rings

These buttermilk onion rings are delicious and highly habit-forming to eat! Try serving these at your next housewarming party.

Ingredients:

2 lg. yellow onions
1 qt. buttermilk
2 c. unsalted cracker meal
2 c. flour
canola oil, for deep-frying

Directions:

1. Peel and slice ½ inch off top and bottom of onions.
2. Slice into rings about ½-inch thick; separate the rings.
3. In large bowl, place buttermilk; dip each ring into buttermilk and coat with flour.
4. Dip flour-coated ring into buttermilk again, then coat with unsalted cracker meal.
5. Place rings onto a wax paper-lined baking sheet.
6. Separate layers with additional sheets of wax paper.
7. Place in airtight plastic bags and freeze. Best if frozen overnight to allow batter to set.
8. At this stage, the amount of coated onion rings you are not using immediately can be placed in an air-tight bag and kept in freezer.
9. Remove from freezer the amount of coated onion rings needed at a time; deep fry in hot oil until golden brown.
10. Remove from hot oil and place on paper towels to drain.
11. Salt, if desired, at serving time.

Shrimp Cocktail with Onion

Once again, this is one of my favorite appetizers. My mom used to make this for my birthday treat when I was young, and I loved it. This shrimp cocktail sauce is excellent. Be sure and select the freshest shrimp you can.

Ingredients:

2 c. chili sauce or ketchup
¼ c. prepared horseradish
½ tsp. white pepper
½ tsp. salt
¼ tsp. dry mustard
1 Tbs. hot sauce
½ c. celery, finely chopped
½ c. onion, finely chopped
2 Tbs. salt
1 gal. water
½ lemon, juiced
20 lg. shrimp in shell
lemon wedges, cut from remaining ½ lemon
fresh lettuce leaves, or shredded lettuce

Directions:

1. In large bowl, combine sauce, horseradish, white pepper, salt, mustard, and hot sauce; blend well.
2. Add celery and onion to sauce; mix well.
3. Place water, salt, and lemon juice in large pot; bring to boil.
4. Add shrimp; cook 3 to 5 minutes until pink color.
5. Remove from heat; drain in colander and chill under cold running water.
6. Peel and devein shrimp.
7. On individual serving plates, arrange shrimp on fresh lettuce leaves or shredded lettuce.
8. Add cocktail sauce, and serve with wedges of fresh lemon.

Crab Stuffed Potatoes

Crab is a great addition to stuffed potatoes and gives a new twist to the old standard of twice-baked potatoes.

Ingredients:

4 lg. white baking potatoes
4 Tbs. butter
½ c. sour cream
4 tsp. onion, finely chopped
1 tsp. salt
½ lb. crabmeat
½ tsp. paprika

Directions:

1. Preheat oven to 375 degrees F.
2. With a fork, prick 4 large baking potatoes.
3. Bake 20 to 25 minutes, or until knife inserts easily into middle of potatoes.
4. Remove from oven; cool to warm.
5. Reduce heat to 350 degrees F.
6. Cut in half lengthwise, being careful not to tear skins, and scoop out insides into bowl; set peels aside.
7. In mixing bowl, combine the insides of potatoes, butter, sour cream, onion, and salt; using hand mixer on low speed for 1 minute, beat until creamy.
8. Carefully fold in crabmeat; gently place mixture back into potato skins to avoid breaking up lumps of crabmeat.
9. Place on baking sheet.
10. Sprinkle with paprika.
11. Bake 15 minutes.
12. Remove from oven and serve while hot.

Italian Bruschetta

This is a wonderful Italian appetizer. Sweet onions make it particularly tasty.

Ingredients:

2 lg. tomatoes, coarsely chopped
½ sweet onion, chopped
2 Tbs. olive oil
1 Tbs. fresh oregano, chopped
1 tsp. fresh basil, chopped
2 tsp. fresh parsley, chopped
½ loaf Italian bread, cut into 1-inch slices
¼ c. Parmesan cheese, freshly grated

Directions:

1. Preheat oven to 400 degrees F.
2. In medium bowl, combine tomatoes, onion, olive oil, oregano, basil, and parsley; mix well.
3. Place bread on a baking sheet; top each slice with tomato mixture; sprinkle with fresh Parmesan cheese.
4. Bake 8 to 10 minutes, or until bottom of bread is browned.
5. Cool 3 to 5 minutes before serving.

Onion Cheese Puffs

These are excellent appetizers and may be prepared through step three of the directions several hours in advance, then spread and place under the broiler right before serving.

Ingredients:

½ sm. yellow onion, chopped
½ c. mayonnaise
5 Tbs. Parmesan cheese, freshly grated
2½ Tbs. fresh parsley, finely chopped
8 slices white bread
salt and pepper, to taste

Directions:

1. In medium bowl, combine mayonnaise, onion, 3 tablespoons of Parmesan cheese, parsley, and salt and pepper to taste.
2. Remove crusts from bread.
3. Cut out rounds with cookie cutter or cut each slice into 4 quarters.
4. Bake on a baking sheet 10 to 15 minutes, or until golden.
5. Remove from oven.
6. Spread 1 teaspoon of the onion mixture onto bread rounds.
7. Sprinkle all rounds with remaining 2 tablespoons of cheese.
8. Brown under broiler for 1 to 2 minutes.
9. Serve while warm.

Sweet Onion Appetizer

This is very easy to make and is delicious served with slices of crusty bread or your favorite crackers.

Ingredients:

1 c. sweet onion, chopped
1 c. Swiss cheese, shredded
1 c. mayonnaise
paprika, for color

Directions:

1. Preheat oven to 375 degrees F.
2. In small bowl, mix onion, cheese, and mayonnaise together.
3. Pour into lightly oiled pie plate.
4. Sprinkle with paprika.
5. Bake 15 to 20 minutes, or until brown and bubbly on top.
6. Cool to warm.
7. Place in a serving bowl.
8. Serve as a dip or spread for your favorite appetizers.

Cheese Ball

This cheese ball makes a great addition to any party or snack time and tastes great served with vegetable sticks or your favorite crackers.

Ingredients:

1 c. pecans, chopped
1 green onion, very finely chopped
¼ c. fresh parsley, finely chopped
1 c. Colby cheese, chopped
1 c. blue cheese, crumbled
1 c. cream cheese, softened
1 tsp. garlic, minced
1 Tbs. Worcestershire sauce
hot pepper sauce, to taste

Directions:

1. In small bowl, combine pecans and parsley; set aside.
2. In large bowl, combine all cheeses, green onion, garlic, and hot sauces to taste; mix well.
3. Cover; chill mixture in refrigerator for 1 hour.
4. Form chilled cheese mixture into ball or log shape; roll in the pecan and parsley mixture.
5. May be stored at this stage; tightly wrap in plastic wrap for several days.
6. Serve with crackers or vegetables.

Did You Know? . . . .

Did you know that the Romans made poultices of onions and barley meal to place over watery eyes? Onions were said to clear the sight by the tears they caused.

Beverages

Table of Contents

Apple, Carrot, and Onion Tonic

This tonic has a spicy bite to it but is so delicious and great for your health that you will want to drink it anyway.

Ingredients:

4 carrots, chopped
1 apple, cored, peeled, chopped
1 pc. gingerroot, peeled, ¼-inch long
1 garlic clove, peeled
½ tsp. onion, chopped
1 dash hot sauce
handful of parsley, to absorb garlic
water

Directions:

1. In blender container, place carrots, apple, and ginger; purée until smooth.
2. Add garlic, onion, hot sauce, and parsley; blend again, adding enough water to liquefy if necessary.
3. Pour into chilled glasses and serve.

Avocado Aperitif

This makes a refreshing summer drink chock full of vitamins and flavor.

Ingredients:

1 med. avocado, peeled, pitted
1 lg. cucumber
½ c. parsley, chopped
1 tsp. sweet onion, grated
2 c. crushed ice
juice of 1 lemon
lemon slices, for garnish
cucumber peel, grated, for garnish

Directions:

1. Grate outside skin of cucumber onto a dish; set aside.
2. Chop remaining cucumber into chunks and place in blender along with avocado.
3. Add parsley, onion, and lemon; blend until smooth.
4. Add crushed ice and blend again.
5. Pour into chilled glasses.
6. Garnish with lemon slices and a bit of grated cucumber peel.

Avocado, Garlic, and Onion Tonic

This makes a cool, healthy, and satisfying drink in the afternoon that will hold one over until dinnertime.

Ingredients:

3 avocados, peeled, pitted
1½ c. vegetable broth
2 tsp. lime juice, fresh
2 garlic cloves
3 Tbs. sweet onion, grated
1 c. light cream
½ tsp. salt
dash nutmeg, for garnish
celery spears, for garnish

Directions:

1. In a blender, purée avocados with a small amount of broth, lime juice, onion, and garlic until smooth.
2. Add remaining broth, cream, and salt to taste.
3. Additional cream or small amount of water can be added if a thinner drink is desired.
4. Place in refrigerator and chill thoroughly.
5. When ready to serve, pour into large chilled serving mugs; add a dash of nutmeg over the top.
6. Add a spear of celery for garnish.

Red Pepper Sunrise

I love red peppers, and they make a very refreshing drink. Serve this drink as an appetizer at your next outdoor barbecue or summer get together.

Ingredients:

1 lg. red bell pepper, halved lengthwise
1 c. crushed ice
⅔ c. buttermilk
1 Tbs. fresh lemon juice
½ tsp. sweet onion, chopped
¼ tsp. hot red pepper flakes, or to taste
paprika
dill pickle spears

Directions:

1. Preheat broiler.
2. Place pepper, with cut sides down on a baking sheet.
3. Broil 4 inches from heat, 10 minutes, until skin is charred.
4. Remove from oven and place in a plastic bag; let sweat until cool.
5. Remove and discard skin and seeds; coarsely chop pepper.
6. Place in a blender along with ice, buttermilk, lemon juice, onion, and red pepper flakes; purée until smooth.
7. Pour into chilled mugs.
8. Garnish with paprika.
9. Add 1 dill pickle spear to each mug.

Yields: 2 mugs.

Onion, Tomato, and Celery Aperitif

This is a healthy and delicious drink any time of the year, but it is really refreshing in the hot summer.

Ingredients:

3 lg. ripe tomatoes
1 small onion, chopped
4 celery stalks with leaves, chopped
½ c. parsley, chopped
1 lime, juiced
½ tsp. celery salt
1 tsp. hot sauce
2 c. crushed ice
grated lime peel, for garnish
celery stalks with leaves, for garnish

Directions:

1. Place tomatoes in blender; purée until smooth.
2. Add onion, celery, parsley, and lime juice; blend until smooth, making sure all tomato seeds are puréed, or if preferred, strain seeds out by pouring liquid through a fine mesh strainer.
3. Add celery salt and hot sauce, to taste.
4. Add crushed ice a little at a time and blend again.
5. Pour into chilled glasses.
6. Place celery stalk in each glass, sprinkle with lime peel and serve immediately.

Yields: 4 servings.

Did You Know?. . . .

Did you know that in desert regions onions were used as a preventative of thirst by travelers and soldiers on the march?

Creamy Onion Yogurt Shake

This is a nutritious, cool drink and a very satisfying snack, especially on a late afternoon during a hot summer when dinner will be served later than usual.

Ingredients:

⅔ c. honey
1½ c. milk
1 sm. sweet onion, chopped
1½ c. lemon or lime yogurt
1 lime, juiced
¼ c. raspberry juice
¼ c. pineapple juice
fresh mint leaves, minced
lime zest

Directions:

1. In a blender, combine honey, milk, yogurt, and onion; purée until smooth.
2. Add lime, raspberry, and pineapple juice, blending well.
3. Cover and chill in refrigerator, to blend flavors.
4. When ready to serve, pour into chilled glasses.
5. Sprinkle mint leaves mixed with the lime zest over top for garnish.

Six Veggie Drink

Cilantro adds a kick to this combination of vegetables in this delicious drink.

Ingredients:

½ c. cilantro
½ cucumber, chopped

½ red or green bell pepper, seeded, chopped
2 med. celery stalks, chopped
6 med. carrots, chopped
2 med. tomatoes, quartered

Directions:

1. In blender, place cilantro, cucumber, pepper, celery, and carrots; purée.
2. Add tomatoes and process according to blender directions to extract juices.
3. Pour into chilled glasses and serve.

Carrot Smoothie

This unique smoothie is also full of vitamins and flavor. Enjoy it as an early morning pick-me-up.

Ingredients:

½ c. soft silken tofu
½ c. carrot juice, chilled
½ c. carrots, chopped
1 c. frozen vanilla yogurt
3 Tbs. frozen orange juice concentrate
1 Tbs. lemon juice
¼ tsp. fresh gingerroot, chopped
¼ tsp. sweet onion, chopped
salt, to taste

Directions:

1. In blender, combine tofu, carrot juice, and carrots.
2. Add frozen yogurt, concentrate, lemon juice, ginger, and onion; salt to taste.
3. Blend until smooth; add more juice if desired.
4. Pour into chilled glasses to serve.

Eight Veggie Drink

This is another delicious and healthy drink made with fresh, raw vegetables. This nonsweet low calorie drink is an excellent energizer.

Ingredients:

1 tomato
½ cucumber
2 carrots
2 celery stalks
2 handfuls fresh spinach leaves
1 red pepper, seeded
1 c. cabbage, chopped
1 green onion, chopped
black pepper or hot sauce (optional)
cucumber slices, for garnish

Directions:

1. Wash all vegetables and chop coarsely.
2. Place a third of the vegetables in blender, purée on high until consistency of juice, continuing to add vegetables in small amounts until all vegetables are blended.
3. Add black pepper or hot sauce to taste, if desired.
4. Pour over ice in tall chilled glasses.
5. Serve with cucumber slice for garnish.

Did You Know? . . . .

Did you know that there are over 380 semi-truck loads of onions consumed each day?

Did you know that the average American eats 21 pounds of onions per year?

Onion Delights Cookbook
A Collection of Onion Recipes
Cookbook Delights Series-Book 8

Breads and Rolls

Table of Contents

Page

Bacon and Onion Rolls

Bacon and onions combine to make a very fragrant and hearty dinner roll. Serve hot out of the oven with butter.

Ingredients:

2 Tbs. yeast
3 c. water, warm, divided
4 tsp. sugar
4 Tbs. butter
8 slices bacon, cooked, crumbled
4 Tbs. green onion, finely chopped
7 c. flour
3 tsp. salt

Directions:

1. Dissolve yeast in ½ cup warm water.
2. Combine remaining water and remaining ingredients in bread maker; knead 15 minutes.
3. Remove from machine; grease lightly.
4. Pinch off dough into balls and place in greased cupcake tins, or divide dough in half and put in round casserole or bread pans.
5. Let rise until double in bulk.
6. Preheat oven to 400 degrees F.
7. Bake 20 to 25 minutes, depending on type of pan used, or until light golden brown.

Caramelized Onion Cheddar Biscuits

These biscuits are delicious and really cheesy. We like them hot out of the oven with butter.

Ingredients:

2 Tbs. butter

½ lg. onion, chopped
1¾ c. flour
1 Tbs. baking powder
¾ tsp. salt
⅓ c. butter, softened
1½ c. Cheddar cheese, divided
½ c. milk
pepper, to taste

Directions:

1. Preheat oven to 400 degrees F.
2. Lightly grease a baking sheet.
3. Place onions in a skillet with 2 tablespoons of butter.
4. Sauté on medium-high heat until browned and butter is about gone.
5. Remove from heat and set aside.
6. In medium bowl, combine flour, baking powder, salt, and pepper.
7. Cut in butter with a pastry blender or 2 knives until mixture resembles coarse crumbs.
8. Stir in 1 cup of cheese.
9. Add milk and caramelized onions; mix just until dry ingredients are moistened.
10. Turn dough out onto floured surface.
11. Knead gently 8 to 10 times.
12. Roll out or pat dough to ½-inch thick; cut with 2½-inch biscuit cutter.
13. Gently press scraps together and pat out, cutting into additional biscuits.
14. Place on prepared baking sheet 2 inches apart.
15. Sprinkle tops with remaining ½ cup cheese.
16. Bake 10 to 12 minutes, or until biscuits are golden brown.
17. Remove from oven and lift onto rack or serve while hot.

Yields: 10 to 12 biscuits.

Baking Powder Biscuits with Onions

These are light and fluffy baking powder biscuits with just a hint of onion flavor. They will enhance any meal and are best when served hot out of the oven with butter.

Ingredients:

- 1 med. onion, peeled, minced
- 1 shallot, peeled, minced
- ⅔ c. butter
- 3 c. flour
- 1 Tbs. baking powder
- 1 tsp. salt
- 1 c. milk, as needed

Directions:

1. Preheat oven to 375 degrees F.
2. Line baking sheet with parchment or wax paper.
3. In a skillet, sauté onions and shallot in 1 tablespoon of the butter until softened, about 5 minutes; set aside to cool.
4. In medium bowl, sift together flour, baking powder, and salt.
5. Cut 9 tablespoons of butter into mixture with 2 knives until mixture resembles coarse meal.
6. Stir in cooled onion mixture; add just enough milk to hold dough together.
7. Transfer to lightly floured surface, and knead 10 times.
8. Roll dough out ¾-inch thick.
9. Cut into 1½-inch squares.
10. Place on baking sheet.
11. Melt and brush remaining butter on biscuit tops.
12. Bake 18 minutes, or until light brown.

Buttermilk Chive Biscuits

This is a really flavorful biscuit to serve with a bowl of homemade soup or stew. It is delicious and light, and also great to use for sandwiches.

Ingredients:

- 2 c. flour
- 2 tsp. baking powder
- ½ tsp. baking soda
- ½ tsp. salt
- ½ c. butter, chilled, cut into sm. pieces
- ¾ c. buttermilk
- 2 Tbs. chives, chopped

Directions:

1. Preheat oven to 375 degrees F.
2. In mixing bowl, sift together flour, baking powder, baking soda, and salt.
3. Add butter; cut in with fork or knives until mixture becomes crumbly.
4. Add buttermilk and chives.
5. Mix just until dry ingredients are moistened.
6. Gather dough into ball, pressing it to hold together; turn out onto a lightly floured surface.
7. Knead gently about 12 times.
8. Pat dough into a circle, keeping it about ½ to ¾-inch thick.
9. Use a 2-inch cookie cutter to cut rounds; place on baking sheet.
10. Bake 15 minutes, or until tops are lightly browned.
11. Remove from oven and lift to serving plate to serve while warm.

Yields: 15 biscuits.

Dried Onion Bagels

These bagels are absolutely scrumptious! They have a dense, chewy texture, like all bagels should, and are perfect for toasting or making sandwiches. Don't be afraid to double the recipe, as they also freeze well.

Ingredients:

¼ c. dried, instant, minced onions
⅓ c. water, warm
1 pkg. yeast
1½ c. water, warm, divided
5 c. flour, approximate
2 tsp. salt
2 Tbs. sugar
1 egg white mixed with 1 Tbs. water, for wash

Directions:

1. Presoak dried onions in ⅓ cup warm water for 10 minutes, drain and press water from onions; set aside.
2. Combine yeast and ½ cup warm water in measuring cup, stirring with fork until dissolved.
3. Sift together 2 cups flour, salt, and sugar in bowl.
4. Add dissolved yeast and remaining 1 cup warm water and half of the soaked onions; beat vigorously with whisk or spoon for 2 minutes.
5. Gradually add enough of remaining flour, ¼ cup at a time, to make soft dough.
6. Turn out of bowl onto floured surface; knead until smooth and elastic, adding as little flour as necessary, for 8 to 10 minutes. Do not skimp on the kneading.
7. Place dough in bowl, cover with plastic wrap, and put in warm place to rise 45 to 60 minutes, or until double in bulk.

8. Punch down dough and divide into 12 equal portions, about 3 to 4 ounces each, weighing dough on kitchen scale for accuracy and size.
9. Form into smooth balls, gently pulling sides of dough down and tucking ends underneath.
10. Place on floured surface; let rest 10 minutes.
11. Using finger or wooden spoon handle, punch a hole in the center of each piece and twirl, or gently widen hole to create bagel shape.
12. Cover with towel and let rest 20 to 30 minutes.
13. Bring to boil, 6 cups of water or enough to make a 4-inch depth of water in wide pan; stir in sugar and salt; reduce heat to simmer.
14. Gently drop 3 or 4 bagels at a time into simmering water; poach first side 2 minutes, turn to cook other side 2 minutes.
15. Remove bagels from water with slotted spoon and place on paper towels to cool.
16. Over sink, brush each bagel with egg white wash.
17. Place bagels on greased baking sheet.
18. Sprinkle with minced or dried onions.
19. Bake in preheated oven at 375 degrees F. for 30 minutes.
20. Note: If you like crispy crust rather than chewy, bake at 375 degrees F. for 15 minutes, then brush on the egg wash and sprinkle with desired topping and return bagels to oven for 2 minutes more.
21. Remove from oven and lift from baking sheet onto wire racks to cool.

Yields: 12 bagels.

Did You Know? . . . .

Did you know that there are 30 calories in a serving of onions?

Onion and Dill Rolls

Onion and dill combine to make a wonderfully flavored treat. Serve hot, right out of the oven.

Ingredients:

2 Tbs. yeast
3 c. water, very warm, divided
4 tsp. sugar
4 Tbs. butter
2 Tbs. dill weed
3 Tbs. onion, minced
7 c. flour
3 tsp. salt
canola oil

Directions:

1. In small bowl, dissolve yeast in ½ cup of the water.
2. Lightly grease muffin tins or loaf pans.
3. In another small bowl, combine remaining water, sugar, butter, dill, onion, and salt.
4. In large bowl, place flour; make a well in center; add combined ingredients in center.
5. Slowly mix flour into wet addition until all of the flour is incorporated.
6. Turn out onto lightly floured surface; knead 15 minutes.
7. Place into oiled bowl, turn to cover with some oil; let rise until double in bulk.
8. Divide dough into rolls or divide dough in half and place into prepared pans.
9. Oil tops and let rise until double in bulk.
10. Bake in preheated oven at 350 degrees F. for 20 minutes for rolls and 35 to 40 minutes for loaves, until light golden brown.

11. Remove from oven and turn out onto wire rack, placing top upright, to cool.

Cheese and Onion Crackers

Cheese and onions add delicious flavor to these easy-to-make crackers.

Ingredients:

½ c. butter, softened
2 c. Cheddar cheese, grated
1½ c. flour
½ tsp. salt
1 Tbs. dried onion
3 Tbs. water

Directions:

1. Preheat oven to 350 degrees F.
2. In medium bowl, combine butter and cheese.
3. Mix together until well blended.
4. Add flour, salt, dried onion, and water to butter mixture.
5. Mix until blended.
6. Form dough into 1-inch balls.
7. Place onto ungreased baking sheets.
8. Gently flatten balls using bottom of drinking glass dipped in flour.
9. Prick each cracker several times with fork.
10. Bake 12 to 15 minutes, until very lightly browned around edges.
11. Remove to wire rack.
12. Cool.

Yields: 36 crackers.

Onion Cheese Bread

This is a somewhat sweet and savory bread. Try it tonight with your family meal.

Ingredients:

2½ c. flour
1 c. whole wheat flour
1 pkg. dry yeast
⅓ c. water, warm
½ c. orange juice
½ c. water
2 Tbs. butter, softened
1 Tbs. onion powder
1 tsp. oregano
1 Tbs. sugar
1 tsp. salt
1¼ c. sharp Cheddar cheese, shredded, divided

Directions:

1. In medium bowl, combine flours and set aside.
2. In large bowl, dissolve yeast in warm water.
3. Add orange juice, water, butter, onion powder, oregano, sugar, salt, and 2 cups of the flour; stir until smooth.
4. Add remaining flour.
5. Turn out onto floured surface and knead until smooth and elastic, about 10 minutes.
6. Cover and let rise until double in bulk.
7. Punch down dough and turn out onto floured surface; press into 8 x 10-inch rectangle.
8. Top with 1 cup of the cheese.
9. Starting at the 8-inch side; roll, pinch ends, and place seam side down in loaf pan.
10. Brush with melted butter and top with remaining cheese.

11. Bake in preheated oven at 375 degrees F. for 45 minutes, or until bread sounds hollow when tapped.
12. Remove from oven and lift from pan onto wire rack to cool.
13. Cool completely before slicing to serve.

Homemade Onion Crackers

These crackers are delicious. The addition of onion makes them a perfect match for your favorite dip.

Ingredients:

1 c. flour
½ tsp. salt
1 Tbs. dried onions
¼ c. milk, more as needed
2 tsp. butter
1 egg, beaten
salt, to taste

Directions:

1. Preheat oven to 375 degrees F.
2. In large bowl, sift together flour and salt; stir in dried onions.
3. In small bowl, mix milk, butter, and egg together.
4. Add to dry ingredients, mixing well; knead if necessary.
5. Roll out dough on baking sheet, making dough very thin and evenly distributed.
6. Score lightly and sprinkle with salt.
7. Bake 10 to 15 minutes, or until brown.
8. Remove from oven and immediately transfer to wire rack to cool and harden.
9. Store any unused crackers in airtight container for up to 6 weeks.

Onion Focaccia

This onion focaccia is so delicious that you can eat it warm out of the oven plain. Use it for sandwiches or even for a thick pizza crust if you like.

Ingredients:

2 c. whole wheat flour
2 c. unbleached bread flour
1 Tbs. instant dry yeast
1 c. water, very warm
6 Tbs. olive oil
1 tsp. salt
1 lb. Vidalia onions, thinly sliced
freshly ground black pepper
cornmeal

Directions:

1. In large bowl, combine both flours together thoroughly.
2. If you prefer, all of one or the other flour may be substituted.
3. Stir yeast into warm water in large mixing bowl, let stand for 10 minutes.
4. Stir in 2 cups flour and beat until mixture is sticky.
5. Turn dough out onto lightly floured surface and knead in remaining flour until dough is smooth and elastic.
6. Place in oiled bowl, cover, and allow rising until double in bulk.
7. Punch down; pour 4 tablespoons of olive oil over dough and sprinkle with the salt.
8. Knead once more, until smooth.
9. Lightly oil a 15-inch pizza pan; dust with cornmeal.
10. Turn out onto lightly floured surface and roll into a circle, 10 to 12-inches in diameter.

11. Place on prepared pan.
12. Let rise until nearly double in bulk.
13. Preheat oven to 425 degrees F.
14. Heat remaining olive oil in frying pan; gently sauté onion 8 to 10 minutes; cool to lukewarm.
15. Spread onions over dough and sprinkle with pepper.
16. Bake for 30 minutes.
17. Remove from oven, cool slightly and then cut into wedges to serve.

Onion Garlic Bubble Bread

This bread is simple to make and absolutely delicious. Try it with butter and honey for a treat.

Ingredients:

1 lb. frozen bread dough, thawed
½ c. butter, melted
½ c. onion, finely chopped
2 garlic cloves, minced
1 tsp. parsley, dried

Directions:

1. Divide bread dough into 24 small balls.
2. In small bowl, combine butter, onion, garlic, and parsley.
3. Dip each ball of dough into butter mixture and place in greased 9-inch bundt pan; pour left over butter mixture over top of rolls.
4. Let rise for 1 hour, or until double in bulk.
5. Bake in preheated oven at 375 degrees F. for approximately 30 minutes, or until golden brown.
6. Remove from oven and lift out onto wire rack to cool.

Sourdough Onion Herb Bread

Nothing can compare to the taste of a warm, freshly baked loaf of sourdough bread right from your own oven.

Ingredients:

2½ c. proofed sourdough starter
1 c. water, warm
8 c. flour, divided
2 tsp. sugar
2 tsp. salt
2 Tbs. dried onion flakes
2 tsp. dry Italian seasoning
cheese, finely shredded
olive oil, for brushing
water, hot

Directions:

1. In large mixing bowl, combine warm water, sourdough starter, and 4 cups of flour.
2. Mix well; cover with clear plastic wrap; let stand in warm place 8 to 12 hours.
3. Stir in salt, sugar, onion flakes, and enough of the remaining flour to form stiff dough; knead until smooth.
4. Cover and let rise in warm place, 2 hours, until double in bulk.
5. Punch down and divide in half.
6. Knead gently until smooth.
7. Shape each half into loaf or round shape; place in greased loaf pans.
8. Cover loaves lightly; let rise in warm place, 1 hour, until puffy and almost doubled in size.
9. Place small pan on shelf, below oven baking rack, and fill with hot water.

10. Bake in preheated oven at 400 degrees F. for 10 minutes.
11. Pull loaves out and leave on rack; brush with olive oil and sprinkle with herbs and cheese.
12. Continue baking 20 to 25 minutes more until loaves are golden brown and sound hollow when tapped.
13. Remove loaves from oven and place on cooling rack until at room temperature.
14. Allow loaf to cool completely.
15. Slice and serve.

Onion Parsley Popovers

These are fragrant and best served warm, right out of the oven. Enjoy with butter and homemade jam.

Ingredients:

1 c. flour
1 tsp. dried parsley
1 tsp. dried onion
1 c. milk
2 lg. eggs, lightly beaten

Directions:

1. Preheat oven to 400 degrees F.
2. Grease 8 ovenproof, 6-ounce custard cups or muffin tin cups.
3. In medium bowl, combine flour, parsley, and onion.
4. Make a well in center of mixture.
5. In small bowl, blend together milk and eggs; pour into well of flour mixture; stir until almost smooth.
6. Spoon batter into cups.
7. Bake 20 minutes; reduce heat to 350 degrees F., bake 15 minutes longer.
8. Remove from oven and lift from cups immediately to wire rack to cool.

Roquefort and Onion Wafers

I love Roquefort cheese, so these are one of my favorite onion crackers.

Ingredients:

1½ c. flour
2½ tsp. cracked pepper
8 oz. Roquefort cheese
¼ c. butter, unsalted
1 c. onion, finely chopped
2 egg yolks, slightly beaten

Directions:

1. In medium bowl, stir flour and pepper together.
2. With pastry blender, cut in cheese and butter until it resembles coarse crumbs.
3. In small bowl, beat egg yolks with fork until well mixed; stir in onions and then add to dry ingredients, mixing until dough begins to cling together.
4. Form dough into a ball; turn out onto a lightly floured surface.
5. Knead dough 10 to 12 strokes; divide dough into 2 pieces and roll into 9-inch logs.
6. Wrap in plastic wrap; refrigerate 2 hours or up to 24 hours.
7. Remove from refrigerator.
8. Preheat oven to 425 degrees F.
9. Cut logs into ¼-inch slices.
10. Place on ungreased baking sheet.
11. Bake 8 to 10 minutes, or until edges turn golden.
12. Remove from oven.
13. Place on wire racks to cool.
14. May be served warm or at room temperature.

Onion Pan Bread

This bread is easy-to-make and goes well with just about any main dish. Be sure to bake enough as your guests will all want seconds.

Ingredients:

3 Tbs. butter, divided
2 c. onions, chopped
2 Tbs. brown sugar
2 c. flour
1 Tbs. baking powder
1 tsp. salt
1 tsp. sugar
1 egg
1 c. milk
¼ c. canola oil

Directions:

1. Preheat oven to 350 degrees F.
2. Grease a 9-inch pie plate with 1 tablespoon of butter; sprinkle bottom with brown sugar.
3. In small skillet, melt remaining butter over medium heat; sauté onions until softened and golden; cool.
4. Spread cooled onions evenly over brown sugar.
5. In large bowl, sift together flour, baking powder, salt, and sugar.
6. In small bowl, combine egg, milk, and oil.
7. Quickly mix wet ingredients into flour mixture.
8. Spread batter over onions.
9. Bake 35 to 40 minutes.
10. Remove from oven; place on wire rack.
11. Cool slightly before slicing to serve.
12. Serve warm with butter and jam if desired.

Sun-Dried Tomato and Onion Bread

Sun-dried tomatoes lend a zesty, Mediterranean flavor to this delicious onion bread.

Ingredients:

4 c. bread flour
1 pinch salt
1 pkg. active dry yeast
2 Tbs. sugar
1 c. water, warm
4 Tbs. olive oil, divided
1 onion, finely chopped
1 garlic clove, crushed
4 oz. sun-dried tomatoes packed in oil, drained
9 lg. basil leaves
1 tsp. coarse sea salt
pepper, to taste
milk, for glazing
basil leaves, for garnish

Directions:

1. In large bowl, sift flour and salt.
2. In small bowl, dissolve yeast and sugar in warm water.
3. Let stand 5 to 10 minutes to activate yeast.
4. Stir 3 tablespoons oil into yeast mixture.
5. Using a wooden spoon, gradually stir yeast mixture into flour to make soft (but not sticky) dough.
6. Turn out and knead on lightly floured surface for 5 minutes, until smooth and elastic.
7. Put dough into oiled medium-size bowl.
8. Cover and let rise in warm place 35 to 40 minutes, until doubled in size.

9. Heat remaining 1 tablespoon olive oil in skillet, adding onion and garlic; cook 3 minutes until softened.
10. Remove skillet from heat and set aside.
11. Turn out dough onto lightly floured surface and cut in half.
12. Roll out to make 2 rectangles of 9 x 12-inches each.
13. Transfer 1 rectangle to baking sheet and prick surface with fork.
14. Spread cooked onion mixture over dough, leaving a ½-inch border around edge.
15. Arrange sun-dried tomatoes and basil leaves over the onion; season with ground pepper.
16. Moisten edges of dough with a little cold water and cover with second sheet of dough.
17. Crimp edges to seal.
18. Using a sharp knife make a lattice pattern on surface of dough.
19. Preheat oven to 450 degrees F.
20. Brush with a little milk to glaze and sprinkle with coarse sea salt and basil; let rise 20 minutes.
21. Bake 25 minutes, until golden brown and underside is firm and lightly colored.
22. Remove from oven, cut into squares.
23. Serve either warm or cold.

Did You Know? . . . .

Did you know the skins of two red onions or yellow storage onions are enough to dye one dozen eggs?

Did you know that Libya boasts the highest per capita consumption of onions per person per year at 66.8 pounds?

Did you know that sulfuric compounds in onions bring tears to your eyes? To cut down on the crying, chill the onion and cut into the root end of the onion last.

Onion Bagels

Onion bagels are always popular. Serve cold as bagel sandwiches or toasted with butter.

Ingredients:

- 2 Tbs. canola oil
- ⅔ c. onion, minced
- 4 Tbs. canola oil
- 2 Tbs. sugar
- ½ tsp. salt
- 1 c. water, hot
- 2 pkg. dry yeast
- 1 egg
- 3¾ c. flour, sifted

Directions:

1. In skillet, over medium heat, sauté onions in 2 tablespoons oil until tender.
2. In bowl, mix oil, sugar, and salt with the hot water.
3. When cooled to lukewarm, add yeast to dissolve.
4. Add egg, onion, and garlic to liquid.
5. Mix in flour, blending well.
6. Knead dough; shape into bagels.
7. Cover and let rise.
8. Preheat oven to 400 degrees F.
9. Drop bagels one at a time into boiling water.
10. Cook for 2 minutes on each side.
11. Remove from water with a slotted spoon; drain.
12. Place on baking sheet.
13. Bake for 15 minutes, or until crisp and golden brown.

Yields: 30 bagels.

Onion Bread

This onion bread has great flavor and is best served warm right out of the oven.

Ingredients:

- 2 c. milk
- 2 pkg. active dry yeast
- ¾ c. water, warm
- 3 Tbs. sugar, divided
- 2½ tsp. salt
- 3 Tbs. butter
- ½ c. dried onion flakes
- 6¼ c. flour

Directions:

1. In small saucepan, warm milk until it bubbles.
2. Remove from heat and cool until lukewarm.
3. In large bowl, stir together yeast, warm water, and 1 tablespoon of sugar; set aside to activate yeast.
4. Add milk, remaining sugar, salt, butter, onion flakes, and 6 cups of flour to the yeast and milk mixture.
5. Combine until dough forms.
6. Turn out onto lightly floured surface; knead until dough is elastic.
7. Place dough in oiled bowl and turn several times to coat; cover and let rise 30 minutes.
8. Place dough into two greased loaf pans; let rise for 30 minutes.
9. Bake in preheated oven at 375 degrees F. for 40 minutes, or until bread sounds hollow when tapped.
10. Remove from oven; turn out of pans onto wire rack.
11. Cool before slicing.

Onion English Loaf

This is an easy bread to make and a great, savory treat for those who love this type of flavorful bread.

Ingredients:

1 pkg. active dry yeast
¼ c. water, very warm
1 c. milk
3 c. bread flour
1½ tsp. sugar
¾ tsp. salt
¼ tsp. baking soda
½ c. onion, chopped
1 Tbs. cornmeal

Directions:

1. In small cup, place yeast in the warm water and dissolve.
2. In small saucepan, warm milk until very warm.
3. In large bowl, sift together 1½ cups of the flour, sugar, salt, and soda.
4. Stir in milk, yeast water, and onion into flour mixture; beat well.
5. Stir in remaining flour, one ½ cup at a time, until stiff batter is formed.
6. Spoon batter into a lightly greased 8 x 4-inch loaf pan sprinkled with cornmeal.
7. Cover and let rise in warm place for 45 minutes until nearly doubled in size.
8. Bake in preheated oven at 400 degrees F. for 25 to 30 minutes, or until golden brown.
9. Remove from oven; turn out of pan immediately.
10. Cool on wire rack right side up.

Onion Soda Crackers

Buttermilk makes these soda crackers extra delicious. Guests are always impressed with homemade crackers.

Ingredients:

- 2 c. flour
- ½ tsp. onion salt
- 1 tsp. dried onion
- 2 tsp. baking powder
- ½ tsp. baking soda
- ¼ c. butter
- ½ c. buttermilk
- 1 lg. egg

Directions:

1. Preheat oven to 400 degrees F.
2. Lightly grease baking sheets.
3. In large bowl, sift together dry ingredients.
4. Cut in butter until mixture is very fine.
5. In small bowl, combine buttermilk and egg.
6. Add to dry ingredients; mix to form dough.
7. Turn out onto lightly floured surface; knead thoroughly.
8. Roll very thin onto prepared baking sheets.
9. Cut into squares or rounds.
10. Prick each cracker with a fork several times.
11. Bake 10 minutes, or until lightly browned.

Did You Know?. . . .

Did you know that Ulysses S. Grant appreciated the antiseptic qualities of onions? In 1864, Grant advised the government, "I will not move my army without onions." Three carloads were shipped to him immediately.

Onion Sesame Crackers

Sesame seeds, whole wheat, and yogurt set these crackers apart from others. These are a great way to enhance your favorite soup or salad.

Ingredients:

1 c. whole wheat flour
1 c. flour
1 tsp. onion salt
1½ tsp. baking powder
¼ c. yogurt
1 Tbs. butter
4 Tbs. sesame seeds
⅝ c. ice water
2 Tbs. dried onion

Directions:

1. Preheat oven to 350 degrees F.
2. Lightly grease a baking sheet.
3. In large bowl, sift together both flours, salt, and baking powder two times; cut in the yogurt.
4. In small saucepan, melt butter. Toast sesame seeds until they are slightly brown.
5. Add to flour mixture.
6. Mix in ice water and dried onion, kneading lightly.
7. On prepared baking sheet, turn out dough and roll to ⅛-inch thickness.
8. Score deeply into squares with knife; prick each square several times with fork.
9. Bake 10 to 15 minutes, or until lightly brown.
10. Remove from oven.
11. Remove crackers immediately to wire rack to cool. Crackers will become crisper as they cool.
12. May be kept up to 6 weeks in airtight container.

Parmesan Onion Crackers

These simple cheese and herb crackers are delicious. They are an elegant addition to your favorite soup, salad, or snack.

Ingredients:

1¾ c. Parmesan cheese, freshly grated from round
¼ c. onion, grated
tarragon, parsley, dill, and/or thyme leaf, to taste

Directions:

1. Preheat oven to 375 degrees F.
2. On a baking sheet, using a 2-inch cookie cutter as a guide, sprinkle 1 tablespoon cheese into the inside of cutter.
3. Using the tip of a spoon, spread cheese as thinly as possible.
4. Repeat, leaving 1 inch between each crisp.
5. Lightly chop herbs and mix them together.
6. Sprinkle a few on each round of cheese, along with a pinch of grated onion.
7. Place baking sheet on center rack of oven.
8. Bake 2 to 3 minutes, making sure the crackers do not brown.
9. Remove very quickly; transfer to a cool surface to help stop the cooking process.
10. Serve when cooled with your favorite soup or salad.

Yields: 25 to 30 crackers.

Did You Know? . . . .

Did you know that onions were consumed by the laborers who built the Great Pyramids of Egypt?

Parmesan, Black Olive, and Onion Crackers

Black olives and Parmesan cheese add delicious flavor to these onion crackers. Bon Appétit!

Ingredients:

2 c. flour
½ lb. Parmesan cheese, grated to measure 2 c.
2 egg yolks
1¼ c. butter, unsalted, melted, cooled
3 Tbs. water
2 Tbs. onion, grated
¼ c. black olives, pitted, chopped

Directions:

1. Preheat oven to 375 degrees F.
2. In large bowl, mix together flour and cheese.
3. In small bowl, beat egg yolks into butter.
4. Add grated onion and mix.
5. Pour egg mixture and water into flour mixture.
6. Stir in olives.
7. Roll batter into balls 1½-inches in diameter.
8. Place on a nonstick baking sheet.
9. Flatten with broad serving spatula.
10. Bake 25 to 30 minutes, or until lightly golden.
11. Remove from oven and immediately lift to wire rack to cool.
12. Store in airtight container for up to 6 weeks.

Did You Know? . . . .

Did you know that according to Pliny, Romans used onions to cure the sting of serpents and onion juice to restore speech to the suddenly voiceless?

Breakfasts

Table of Contents

Breakfast Burritos

Breakfast is a great way to start your day, and incorporating onions into your recipe adds great flavor, and also contains anti-cancer, anti-inflammatory, and anti-cholesterol components as an added benefit.

Ingredients:

6 strips bacon
1½ c. potatoes, cooked, peeled
½ c. onion, chopped
1 garlic clove, minced
1 can black beans, drained, rinsed (15 oz.)
2 Tbs. canned green chilies, diced
1 Tbs. butter
6 lg. eggs, lightly beaten
6 flour tortillas (8-inch)
¾ c. red chili sauce
¾ c. green chili sauce
¾ c. Cheddar cheese, shredded

Directions:

1. In large skillet, fry bacon just until crisp. Drain, reserving 1 tablespoon of drippings in pan.
2. Crumble bacon and return to pan; add potatoes, onions, and garlic.
3. Cover; cook 10 minutes, or until potatoes start to brown, stirring occasionally.
4. Add black beans and chilies; heat through.
5. Preheat oven to 350 degrees F.
6. Meanwhile, in another large skillet, heat butter, tilting to cover surface.
7. Pour in eggs and cook, stirring frequently, just until barely set (eggs will continue to cook within burritos).
8. Combine with the bacon and potato mixture.
9. Lay tortillas out flat on work surface.

10. Divide filling evenly among tortillas and roll up; place seam side down in greased baking dish.
11. Spoon green chili sauce over half of all tortillas.
12. Spoon red chili sauce over other half of tortillas.
13. Bake 20 to 25 minutes, or until heated through.
14. Top with cheese, bake 4 to 5 minutes more, or until cheese is melted; cut in half.

Apple Sausage Breakfast Ring

This is a delicious breakfast dish that can be made ahead for a leisurely breakfast or brunch. Fill the center of the ring with scrambled eggs right before serving, and the meal is complete!

Ingredients:

2 lb. lean bulk sausage, unseasoned
2 lg. eggs
1½ c. buttery or club crackers, crushed
1 apple, peeled, cored, grated
½ c. onion, minced
¼ c. milk
salt and pepper, to taste

Directions:

1. In large mixing bowl, combine sausage, eggs, and crackers; break apart the sausage pieces.
2. Add apple, onion, milk, and salt and pepper to taste; blend well.
3. Press mixture into ring mold lined with wax paper or plastic wrap.
4. Cover and place in refrigerator; chill overnight.
5. Unmold and remove paper; place ring onto a baking sheet with raised edges.
6. Bake in preheated oven at 300 degrees F. for 1 hour.
7. Remove from oven, let set for 8 minutes before serving.

Eggs Benedict with Green Onions

My children have made this for me on Mother's Day, and it is an enjoyable classic.

Ingredients:

6 slices cooked ham or Canadian bacon
3 English muffins, halved
⅓ tsp. butter
2 Tbs. green onion, finely chopped
6 eggs
1 truffle or large mushroom, sliced

Directions:

1. Toast English muffin halves.
2. Poach eggs gently; while poaching, sauté slices of cooked ham briefly in butter.
3. On individual serving plates, place each ham slice on a toasted English muffin half; top each with 1 poached egg and green onions.
4. If desired, garnish with truffle or mushroom slice.
5. Serve immediately.

Ham Stuffed Onion Breakfast Biscuits

This is a wonderful recipe to use when you are having a special occasion to celebrate, and is delicious served as a leisurely breakfast or brunch.

Ingredients for dish:

1 Tbs. butter
½ med. onion, finely diced
1 garlic clove, finely minced
1 lb. cooked ham, diced
1 Tbs. fresh parsley, chopped

1 pinch dried thyme
12 hot biscuits, split in half
fresh parsley sprigs, for garnish

Ingredients for cheese sauce:

1 c. butter
1 c. flour
1 tsp. salt
½ tsp. pepper
2 qt. milk, cold
¾ c. American or processed cheese, grated

Directions for cheese sauce:

1. In small saucepan, over medium heat, melt butter.
2. When butter is melted and pan is hot, add flour. Stir briskly with a wooden spoon until smooth.
3. Add salt and pepper.
4. Gradually stir in cold milk, stirring briskly all the while, until it is all added.
5. Continue to cook, while stirring, for 10 minutes; mixture will continue to thicken.
6. Add grated cheese after 10 minutes of cooking, and continue stirring until cheese is melted and sauce is at desired thickness.
7. Add to ham mixture in order called for.

Directions for dish:

1. In a cast iron skillet, sauté onion and garlic in butter until golden brown.
2. Add ham and seasonings; stir in cheese sauce and keep warm.
3. Arrange open biscuits on serving plates.
4. Place a ladleful of ham and cheese mixture in the center of each biscuit, garnish with parsley sprigs, and serve at once.

Omelet Spanish Style

The Spanish omelet is a classic that makes for a very hearty breakfast.

Ingredients:

1 c. olive oil
5 med. baking potatoes, peeled, sliced
⅛ tsp. salt, or to taste
½ yellow onion, chopped
3 garlic cloves, minced
5 eggs
salt, to taste
lemon juice, to taste

Directions:

1. In a 9-inch skillet, heat oil; add potato slices carefully to avoid oil splatter.
2. Try to keep potato slices separated so they will not stick together.
3. Cook, turning occasionally, over medium heat for 5 minutes.
4. Add onions and garlic; cook until potatoes are tender.
5. Drain into colander, leaving 3 tablespoons of oil in the skillet.
6. In large bowl, whisk eggs with a pinch of salt.
7. Add potatoes, and stir to coat with egg.
8. Pour into very hot oil in the skillet, spreading evenly to completely cover skillet base.
9. Reduce heat to medium; continue to cook, shaking pan frequently, until mixture is halfway set.
10. Use plate to cover skillet; invert omelet away from the hand holding plate, so as not to burn your hand with escaping oil.

11. Add 1 tablespoon oil back to pan; slide omelet back into skillet on its uncooked side.
12. Cook until completely set.
13. Remove from heat; allow omelet to cool slightly; then cut into wedges.
14. Season with salt and sprinkle with lemon juice to taste.
15. Serve while hot with sour cream or salsa if desired.

Onion and Cheese Omelet

This is a flavorful omelet. Use your favorite onions and enjoy.

Ingredients:

6 eggs
½ c. Cheddar cheese, grated
¾ c. mushrooms, sliced, fresh or canned
4 Tbs. green onion, diced
4 Tbs. white onion, diced
1 Tbs. onion powder
½ c. pan sausage, cooked, crumbled
salt, to taste

Directions:

1. In medium bowl, whisk eggs; add salt to taste.
2. Lightly spray a medium skillet with cooking spray.
3. Heat until hot and add eggs.
4. Cook until almost done all the way through, then place cheese, mushrooms, and onions onto half of the top.
5. Add crumbled sausage; sprinkle with onion powder and salt, and fold other half over this.
6. Turn off heat; let cheeses melt completely for 1 to 2 minutes.
7. Slip out of pan onto serving dish; serve immediately.

Spicy Breakfast Patty-Cakes

This recipe is nice as it is, but it can be made even better by adjusting the seasonings to your personal preference.

Ingredients:

1¼ lb. ground turkey
½ c. onion, minced
¼ c. fresh basil, chopped
¼ c. fresh parsley, chopped
2 garlic cloves, minced
1 tsp. salt
½ tsp. thyme leaves, dried
½ tsp. ground ginger
½ tsp. dried red pepper flakes
2 Tbs. dried bread crumbs
1 egg, lightly beaten
2 Tbs. canola oil
freshly ground pepper, to taste

Directions:

1. In large mixing bowl, combine turkey, onion, basil, parsley, garlic, and salt; mix just until blended.
2. Add thyme, ginger, red pepper flakes, bread crumbs, and egg, mixing until completely blended; cover and refrigerate 1 hour.
3. Divide mixture into 12 portions; shape into patties 2 to 3-inches in diameter.
4. Heat oil in large skillet; over medium heat, brown patties on both sides, 2 minutes per side.
5. Reduce heat to medium-low, cover skillet and continue cooking.
6. Turn patties occasionally until crisp and cooked through, 6 minutes; serve immediately with freshly ground black pepper to taste.

7. Try serving with scrambled eggs or along side of pancakes or waffles.

Mini Green Onion Pancakes

These savory pancakes make a great side dish for any egg breakfast or even as a side dish when serving roasted meats for dinner.

Ingredients:

2 c. flour
1 c. water
4 stalks green onion, cut into ½-inch pieces
salt
canola oil

Directions:

1. In large bowl, mix flour with water to form dough, cover and let dough rest for 2 hours.
2. Divide dough into 4 portions; work with only 1 piece of dough at a time.
3. Place on a lightly floured surface and flatten dough with rolling pin to 9-inches in diameter.
4. Continue rolling and stretching dough until it is very thin.
5. Brush dough with oil, sprinkle with salt and green onion.
6. Roll dough sheet into a log shape and slice into 1-inch thick pieces.
7. Continue same procedure as above for the other 3 portions of dough.
8. Sauté each batch in pan until done, flipping to cook both sides; cover and keep warm.
9. Best when served warm; reheat before serving if necessary.

Cheddar Strata with Grilled Onions

This dish is so easy to make ahead that you will be able to have it ready for your company or a potluck.

Ingredients:

- 1 tsp. canola oil
- 2 med. onions, chopped
- 8 slices rye bread
- 2 Tbs. Dijon mustard
- 2½ c. Cheddar cheese, shredded
- 1 lg. tomato, seeded, coarsely chopped
- 1½ c. milk
- 4 eggs

Directions:

1. Preheat oven to 325 degrees F.
2. Heat oil in 10-inch nonstick skillet over medium-high heat.
3. Sauté onions in oil, 6 to 8 minutes, stirring frequently, until golden brown; remove from heat.
4. Trim crusts from bread; spread mustard on 1 side of each bread slice.
5. Arrange 4 slices, mustard sides up, in a greased 8 x 8 x 2-inch baking dish.
6. Divide 2 cups of cheese, tomato, and cooked onions into 4 portions; layer in that order on bread in baking dish.
7. Cover with remaining bread, mustard side down.
8. Beat milk and eggs until well-blended; pour evenly over bread.
9. Bake 1 hour, or until center is set and bread is golden brown.
10. Remove from oven; sprinkle with the remaining ½ cup cheese.
11. Let stand 10 minutes before cutting to serve.

Soufflé Omelet with Brie, Mushrooms, and Onions

This is a delightfully rich and flavorful breakfast omelet. Try out this recipe on your next overnight guests.

Ingredients:

4 lg. eggs, separated, whites reserved
1 pinch salt and pepper
2 tsp. fresh parsley, chopped
4 tsp. cream
1 Tbs. butter
½ c. mushrooms, sliced, sautéed
¼ c. onions, chopped, sautéed
4 Tbs. Brie cheese, roughly chopped
1 orange with peel on, sliced

Directions:

1. Preheat oven to 350 degrees F.
2. In small bowl, beat egg yolk until thick and light in color.
3. Add cream, salt, pepper, and parsley.
4. Beat egg whites until they form peaks.
5. Fold into yolk mixture.
6. Gently fold in mushrooms and onions.
7. Pour into a hot, buttered, cast iron pan.
8. Cook slowly, until omelet puffs up and is firm on the bottom.
9. Place in oven and bake for 3 minutes.
10. Sprinkle cheese on top and bake for an additional 2 minutes.
11. Remove from oven and slide onto serving platter.
12. Cut into wedges.
13. Garnish with orange slices.

Breakfast Volcanoes

This dish is similar to eggs benedict but uses scrambled eggs and veggies in place of poached eggs. Try this recipe the next time you are hungry for a change of pace in your breakfast.

Ingredients for hollandaise sauce:

3 egg yolks, reserve whites
1 Tbs. cold water
½ c. butter, room temperature
¼ tsp. salt
1 tsp. lemon juice, or to taste

Ingredients for dish:

2 English muffins
4 slices tomato, thick sliced
2 Tbs. onion, chopped
2 Tbs. green pepper, chopped
1 Tbs. butter, room temperature
5 lg. eggs, plus 3 reserved whites, beaten

Directions for hollandaise sauce:

1. In top of a double boiler, over low heat, combine egg yolks with water.
2. Beat with a wire whisk continuously until fluffy; do not allow water to boil.
3. Add a few spoonfuls of butter to the mixture; beat continually until butter has melted and the sauce starts to thicken.
4. Care should be taken that the water in the bottom of the boiler never boils.
5. Continue adding butter, in very small amounts, stirring constantly.
6. Add salt and lemon juice.
7. For a lighter texture, beat in a tablespoon of hot water if desired.

8. Remove boiler and pan from heat; cover and set aside, leaving over warm boiler.

Directions for dish:

1. Split and toast English muffins; place on serving plate and lay one slice of tomato on each muffin.
2. In small skillet, sauté onions and green pepper in butter until soft.
3. Add beaten reserved whites and eggs; scramble until cooked.
4. Top tomato slices with cooked scrambled egg mixture and 3 tablespoons of the reserved Hollandaise sauce.
5. Serve immediately.

Onion and Potato Pancakes

These are savory, hearty pancakes that go well with fried eggs and sausage.

Ingredients:

8 med. potatoes, grated, rinsed
2 med. onions, grated
6 eggs
6 Tbs. flour
salt, to taste
butter or canola oil, for frying

Directions:

1. Drain or press potatoes between paper towels to remove liquid.
2. In small bowl, mix onion, eggs, flour, and salt to taste.
3. Add mixture to potatoes and mix well.
4. In skillet, with enough butter or oil to thoroughly cover bottom of pan, fry 2 tablespoons of mixture at a time, spreading out thinly so potatoes will fry crisp.
5. Remove from pan and serve while hot.

Breakfast Lasagna

Are you looking for a change of pace for breakfast? Try this dish on a weekend and brighten up everyone's day with a hearty, savory dish. Serve with fresh fruit compote to complete the meal.

Ingredients:

1 pkg. lasagna noodles
1 lb. ricotta cheese
2 eggs
6 Tbs. butter
6 Tbs. flour
3 c. milk
½ tsp. dry mustard
¼ tsp. nutmeg
1 tsp. salt
2 Tbs. red wine
½ c. onion, chopped
4 garlic cloves, finely chopped
1 Tbs. olive oil
1½ tsp. tomato paste
1 lb. cooked ham, thinly sliced
½ lb. Gruyere cheese, grated
½ lb. mozzarella cheese, grated
½ lb. Parmesan cheese, freshly grated
fresh parsley, chopped

Directions:

1. Preheat oven to 350 degrees F.
2. Lightly grease a 9 x 13 x 2-inch baking dish.
3. Prepare noodles according to package directions; set aside.
4. Mix ricotta cheese with eggs.
5. To prepare white sauce: Melt butter in medium saucepan.
6. Add flour, stirring until smooth.

7. Whisk in milk slowly.
8. On medium-low heat, cook until sauce is smooth and thickened.
9. Add dry mustard, nutmeg, and salt.
10. Stir in wine and half of the Parmesan cheese.
11. In small skillet, in olive oil sauté garlic and chopped onion.
12. Mix in tomato paste.
13. Add this mixture to the white sauce.
14. Layer half of the ingredients into prepared baking dish starting with a thin layer of sauce.
15. Follow with a layer of noodles, followed by the ricotta cheese and egg mixture, ham, Gruyere, and mozzarella cheese.
16. Top with sauce and Parmesan cheese.
17. Repeat, steps 10 and 11 using the remaining half of ingredients, starting with noodles, and ending with sauce and Parmesan cheese.
18. Sprinkle with parsley.
19. Bake 35 to 45 minutes.
20. Remove from oven.
21. Let stand for 10 minutes before serving.

Did You Know? . . . .

Did you know that you can apply roasted onions to the chest to relieve coughs?

Did you know that the weight of the largest onion ever grown was 10 lbs. 12 oz. by V. Throup of Silsden, England?

Did you know that onions have been with us since the beginning of time? Biblically and historically, they have the attributes of a health-giving, disease-preventing substance.

Potato, Apple, and Onion Hash

Potatoes, apples, and onions together make an interesting combination. Be sure to use a tart apple such as Granny Smith or McIntosh. Serve with a slice of fried ham for breakfast, lunch, or dinner. Delicious!

Ingredients:

2 Tbs. olive oil
1 sm. onion, diced
2 lg. potatoes, peeled, diced
2 tart apples, peeled, cored, diced
1 Tbs. fresh thyme leaves
1 Tbs. butter
salt and pepper, to taste

Directions:

1. In a nonstick 12-inch skillet, heat oil and sauté onions over medium heat for 5 minutes, or until translucent.
2. Add potatoes; sauté 6 to 8 minutes, or until half cooked.
3. Add apples, thyme, and butter.
4. Season with salt and pepper to taste.
5. Cook 10 minutes, or until lightly browned and cooked through.
6. Place on serving plates.
7. Add ham or sausage along with toast or muffins to complete your breakfast.

Did You Know? . . . .

Did you know that you can inhale freshly cut onions to clear your nasal passages?

Cakes

Table of Contents

Sweet Onion and Apple Upside-Down Cake

This cake is surprisingly sweet and moist. Serve with French vanilla ice cream for a delicious and unusual dessert.

Ingredients for bottom:

- 1 med. sweet onion, peeled, sliced into 1-inch strips
- 8 Granny Smith apples, peeled, sliced into 1-inch slices
- ⅓ c. butter
- ¾ c. brown sugar, packed
- powdered sugar

Ingredients for batter:

- 4 egg whites
- ¾ c. plus 2 Tbs. flour
- 1½ tsp. baking powder
- 5 oz. milk
- ¾ c. plus 2 Tbs. sugar

Directions for bottom and batter:

1. Preheat oven to 350 degrees F.
2. Spray two baking sheets with nonfat cooking spray.
3. Place onions on baking sheet and apple slices on another.
4. Bake 1 hour, or until caramelized.
5. Bake apples for 4 to 5 minutes; remove from oven and set aside.
6. Melt butter in 10-inch skillet.
7. Add brown sugar; stir with wooden spoon until dissolved.
8. Remove pan from heat, add caramelized onions, and set aside.

9. In large bowl of electric mixer, beat egg whites until fluffy.
10. In medium bowl, mix together flour, sugar, and baking powder.
11. Fold into egg whites alternately with the milk.
12. Spray a 9-inch baking pan with cooking spray; line with parchment paper.
13. Spread brown sugar and onion mixture on the parchment paper.
14. Place sliced apples over onions.
15. Press down to fill gaps between apples.
16. Cover with batter.
17. Bake 45 minutes, or until toothpick inserted in center comes out clean.
18. Remove from oven; cool to room temperature.
19. Reverse pan onto serving tray.
20. Remove parchment paper.
21. Lightly dust with powdered sugar.

Yields: 8 servings.

Did You Know? . . . .

Did you know as a home remedy, you can use syrup of honey and onion juice will help chest congestion?

Quotes . . . .

Banish the onion from the kitchen and the pleasure flies with it. Its presence lends color and enchantment to the most modest dish; its absence reduces the rarest delicacy to hopeless insipidity, and dinner to despair.
-Elizabeth Robbins Pennell – American columnist

"This is every cook's opinion
No savory dish without an onion,
But lest your kissing should be spoiled
Your onions must be boiled."
-Jonathan Swift (1667-1745)

Chocolate Onion Fudge Cake

Here is a moist, delicious cake that the whole family will enjoy, especially those chocolate lovers.

Ingredients for cake:

3½ c. flour
2 Tbs. baking powder
½ c. cocoa
1 tsp. salt
1 c. butter
2⅔ c. sugar
2 c. milk
4 tsp. vanilla extract
½ c. sweet onions, finely chopped
2 c. nuts, chopped

Ingredients for sauce:

2 c. sugar
2 c. brown sugar, packed
¾ c. cocoa
1 tsp. salt
6 c. water, boiling
whipping cream, whipped

Directions for cake:

1. Preheat oven to 350 degrees F.
2. Lightly grease two 9 x 13 x 2-inch baking pans.
3. In medium bowl, sift together flour, baking powder, cocoa, and salt; set aside.
4. In large bowl, cream butter with sugar until light and fluffy.
5. Add flour mixture alternately with milk to creamed ingredients.
6. Stir just enough to blend.
7. Fold in vanilla, onions, and nuts.
8. Spread batter into prepared pans and set aside.

Directions for sauce:

1. In medium bowl, combine sugar, brown sugar, cocoa, and salt; sprinkle over batter.
2. Pour boiling water over batter; do not mix in.
3. Bake 50 minutes, or until cake is firm to the touch.
4. Remove from oven; cool to lukewarm.
5. Cut into 2-inch squares.
6. Top with whipped cream, if desired.

Sweet Onion and Carrot Cupcakes

This is an unusual combination, but it makes a wonderfully delicious cupcake. Frost with vanilla frosting, for a really tasty treat.

Ingredients:

2 eggs
1½ c. honey
½ c. butter
8 oz. fresh tofu, drained
2 tsp. vanilla extract
2 tsp. lemon juice
2 c. whole wheat flour
2 tsp. baking soda
2 tsp. nutmeg
1 c. carrots, finely shredded
½ c. sweet onion, finely chopped
½ c. raisins, chopped
1 c. walnuts or pecans, chopped

Directions:

1. Preheat oven to 375 degrees F.
2. In large mixing bowl, beat together eggs, honey, butter, tofu, vanilla, and lemon juice.
3. In small bowl, sift together flour, baking soda, and nutmeg; add to egg mixture and beat until smooth.
4. Fold in carrots, onions, raisins, and nuts, mixing just enough to incorporate.
5. Line two ½-inch muffin pans with paper baking cups; fill ⅔ full with batter.
6. Bake 20 minutes, or until done.

Amish Onion Cake

This traditional Amish recipe is quite tasty, and it is great for picnics.

Ingredients:

3-4 med. sweet onions, chopped
2 c. butter, divided
1 Tbs. poppy seeds
1½ tsp. salt
1½ tsp. paprika
1 tsp. black pepper, coarsely ground
4 c. flour
½ c. cornstarch
1 Tbs. baking powder
1 Tbs. sugar
1 Tbs. brown sugar
5 eggs
¾ c. milk
¾ c. sour cream

Directions:

1. Preheat oven to 350 degrees F.
2. Lightly grease a 10-inch springform baking pan.
3. In large skillet, cook onions in ½ cup butter over low heat for 10 minutes.
4. Stir in poppy seeds, salt, paprika, and pepper.
5. Cook until golden brown, stirring occasionally.
6. Remove from heat and set aside.
7. In large bowl, combine flour, cornstarch, baking powder, and both sugars.
8. Cut in 1¼ cups butter until mixture resembles coarse crumbs.
9. Melt remaining butter.
10. In another bowl, whisk eggs, milk, sour cream, and melted butter.
11. Make a well in dry ingredients; stir in egg mixture just until moistened.

12. Spread into prepared pan; spoon onion mixture over dough.
13. Place pan on baking sheet.
14. Bake 35 to 40 minutes, or until inserted toothpick comes out clean.
15. Serve warm.

Onion Cake

Try this delicious easy-to-make onion cake.

Ingredients:

3 strips bacon, diced
4 med. onions, finely chopped
3 Tbs. butter
½ c. sour cream
1 Tbs. flour
½ tsp. salt
3 eggs, beaten
1 roll refrigerated crescents rolls (8 oz.)

Directions:

1. Preheat oven to 375 degrees F.
2. Lightly grease a 9-inch square baking pan.
3. In a skillet cook bacon until crisp; drain.
4. In the same skillet, cook onions in butter until tender; cool.
5. In a mixing bowl, combine sour cream, flour, and salt; add eggs.
6. Stir in bacon and onions; set aside.
7. Separate crescent roll dough into four rectangles.
8. Pat dough into the bottom and 1 inch up sides of prepared pan; pinch edges together to seal.
9. Pour onion mixture over dough.
10. Bake 30 minutes, or until the topping is set and crust is golden.
11. Cool slightly before cutting into small squares.

Apple Onion Scandinavian Cake

This is a moist, spicy cake with lots of nuts. Scandinavians value the patience of waiting one week for the flavors to blend.

Ingredients:

- 3 c. flour
- 2 tsp. baking soda
- 2½ tsp. cinnamon
- 2 tsp. allspice
- 1 c. sugar
- ⅔ c. butter, melted
- 2 eggs, beaten
- 3 tsp. vanilla extract
- 1 tsp. cardamom
- 3 lg. tart apples, chopped
- 1 lg. sweet onion, chopped
- 1½ c. nuts, chopped

Directions:

1. Preheat oven to 350 degrees F.
2. Lightly grease and flour two 5 x 8-inch loaf pans.
3. In medium bowl, sift together flour, baking soda, cinnamon, and allspice.
4. In large bowl, combine sugar, butter, eggs, vanilla, and cardamom; cream until fluffy.
5. Add dry ingredients to the creamed mixture; stir only until blended.
6. Gently fold in apples, onions, and nuts.
7. Spoon into prepared loaf pans.
8. Bake 45 to 50 minutes, or until inserted toothpick comes out clean.
9. Remove from oven; let stand for 10 minutes and turn out onto wire rack to cool.

10. Wrap and refrigerate for a week to blend flavors before serving.
11. Will keep up to 3 months frozen.

Sweet Onion Cake

This is a basic sweet onion cake. The flavor is sweet with just a hint of a bite, and the texture is very moist.

Ingredients:

2 c. flour
2 tsp. baking powder
1 tsp. salt
1½ c. sweet onions, chopped
4 Tbs. butter
1½ c. sugar
¼ c. butter
⅓ c. shortening
3 eggs
1 c. milk

Directions:

1. Preheat oven to 350 degrees F.
2. Grease and flour two 9-inch round baking pans.
3. In large bowl, sift together flour, baking powder, and salt; set aside.
4. In heavy skillet, melt 4 tablespoons butter.
5. Sauté onions until lightly crisp but not brown; cool.
6. In large bowl, cream sugar with butter and shortening; add eggs and beat until fluffy.
7. Add flour mixture alternately with milk; stir in sautéed onions and spoon into prepared pans.
8. Bake 30 minutes, or until inserted toothpick comes out clean.
9. Cool in pans, 10 minutes then turn out onto wire rack.

Chocolate Sweet Onion Cake

This is a unique dessert. The chocolate does camouflage the onions, but the onions are sweetened by the process of being sautéed. Try this on your guests without discussing the ingredients, and see if they can taste the onions.

Ingredients for cake:

1½ c. Walla Walla or Vidalia sweet onions, chopped
4 Tbs. butter
2 c. flour
2 tsp. baking powder
1 tsp. salt
1½ c. sugar
¼ c. butter
⅓ c. shortening
4 sq. sweet baker's chocolate
3 eggs, beaten
1 c. milk

Ingredients for icing:

2 Tbs. flour
½ c. milk
½ c. butter
½ c. sugar
½ tsp. vanilla extract

Directions for cake:

1. Preheat oven to 350 degrees F.
2. Lightly grease and flour two 9-inch baking pans.
3. In heavy skillet, melt 4 tablespoons butter.
4. Sauté onions until transparent but not brown; place in mixing bowl to cool.

5. In medium bowl, sift together flour, baking powder, and salt.
6. In large bowl, cream sugar with ¼ cup butter and ⅓ cup shortening until fluffy.
7. Melt chocolate on low in microwave and add to mixture.
8. Add beaten eggs and beat slowly to blend well.
9. Add flour mixture and milk alternately; beat for 3 minutes.
10. Fold in the sautéed onions and stir well.
11. Pour into prepared pans.
12. Bake 30 minutes, or until inserted toothpick comes out clean.
13. Cool in pans for 10 minutes.
14. Turn out on wire rack and cool completely.
15. Frost with creamed icing.

Directions for icing:

1. In small saucepan, boil flour and milk together until thick.
2. Set aside to cool.
3. In small bowl, cream butter, sugar, salt, and vanilla.
4. Beat into flour and milk mixture until creamy and light.
5. Ice cooled cake and serve.

Did You Know? . . . .

Did you know that the yellow onion is the most common onion? Approximately 88 percent of the crops are yellow onions.

Quotes . . . .

An onion can make people cry, but there has never been a vegetable invented to make them laugh.
-Will Rogers (1879-1935)

Peach and Onion Upside-Down Cake

This is a light and delicious cake all by itself, but it is even better served with a scoop of vanilla ice cream.

Ingredients:

1 c. brown sugar
2 Tbs. butter
6 fresh peaches, peeled, halved
1 c. pecan halves
2½ c. flour
1 tsp. baking soda
½ tsp. salt
1 tsp. cinnamon
½ tsp. ground nutmeg
1 c. butter
1½ c. sugar
2 eggs
1 tsp. vanilla extract
1 tsp. almond extract
1 c. sour cream
1 med. sweet onion, finely chopped
vanilla ice cream (optional)

Directions:

1. Preheat oven to 350 degrees F.
2. In small saucepan, over low heat, melt brown sugar with 2 tablespoons butter, until sugar is dissolved.
3. Pour mixture into a 9 x 13-inch baking dish; when cooled, arrange peach halves, cut sides up, in pan; place whole pecan halves between each peach half.
4. Combine flour, baking soda, salt, and spices.
5. In small bowl, beat butter with sugar.
6. Add eggs and both extracts; beating well.
7. Stir in flour mixture by thirds, alternating with sour cream by thirds; fold in onions.
8. Spread batter over peaches.
9. Bake 50 to 55 minutes, or until inserted toothpick comes out clean.
10. Remove from oven; turn out and place onto serving plate to cool.

11. Scrape any sugar mixture that may remain in bottom of pan, over the cake.
12. Cut into squares and serve with ice cream.

Sweet Onion Brown Sugar Cake

The butter and brown sugar make this sweet onion cake an extremely delicious dessert.

Ingredients:

- 4 Tbs. butter
- 2½ c. sweet onions, chopped
- 2½ c. flour
- 2 tsp. baking powder
- 1 tsp. salt
- 1 c. light brown sugar, firmly packed
- ½ c. butter
- ¼ c. shortening
- 3 eggs
- 1 c. sour cream
- ½ tsp. baking soda

Directions:

1. Preheat oven to 350 degrees F.
2. Grease and flour a 9 x 13-inch baking pan.
3. In skillet, melt 4 tablespoons butter, sauté chopped onions, until lightly crisp.
4. In large bowl, sift flour, baking powder, and salt.
5. In small bowl, cream sugar, butter, and shortening until fluffy. Beat eggs in one at a time.
6. Mix the baking soda into the sour cream; blend well.
7. Add to creamed mixture alternately with the dry ingredients; beat 3 to 4 minutes until well blended.
8. Stir in sautéed onions mixing well.
9. Spoon into prepared baking pan.
10. Bake 35 to 40 minutes.
11. Remove from oven and place on rack.
12. When cooled, cut into squares and serve plain or frost with creamed icing.

Vanilla Sweet Onion Cake

The onions become sweet after sautéing, and they add a flavorful taste to this unusual cake.

Ingredients for cake:

1½ c. sweet onions, chopped
4 Tbs. butter
2 c. flour
2 tsp. baking powder
1 tsp. salt
1½ c. sugar
¼ c. butter
1 Tbs. vanilla extract
3 eggs
⅓ c. shortening
1 c. milk

Ingredients for icing:

2 Tbs. flour
½ c. milk
½ c. butter
½ c. sugar
½ tsp. vanilla extract

Directions for cake:

1. Preheat oven to 350 degrees F.
2. Lightly grease and flour two 9-inch round baking pans.
3. In heavy skillet, melt 4 tablespoons butter.
4. Sauté onions until lightly crisp, but not brown.
5. In large bowl, sift together flour, baking powder, and salt.
6. In small bowl, cream sugar with remaining butter and shortening.

7. Beat until fluffy.
8. Add eggs and vanilla; blend well.
9. Add flour mixture alternately with milk to the creamed mixture; beat for 3 minutes.
10. Mix in sautéed onions thoroughly.
11. Pour into prepared baking pans.
12. Bake 30 minutes, or until inserted toothpick comes out clean.
13. Cool in pans 10 minutes.
14. Turn out onto wire rack and cool completely.
15. Frost in layers with creamed icing.

Directions for icing:

1. In small saucepan, combine flour and milk.
2. Boil until thick; cool.
3. In small bowl, cream together butter, sugar, salt, and vanilla.
4. Beat into flour and milk mixture until fluffy.
5. Ice cake and serve.

Mushroom, Apple, and Potato Cake

This cake is delicious and boasts many flavors. Enjoy!

Ingredients:

- 3 Tbs. olive oil, divided
- 1 lb. mushrooms, portobello and/or cremini, stems discarded and caps chopped
- 1 med. onion, finely chopped
- 1 Granny Smith or other tart apple
- 1 tsp. fresh thyme, chopped
- 1 tsp. salt, divided
- ¾ tsp. black pepper, divided
- 1 lb. yellow potatoes

Directions:

1. In 10-inch cast iron skillet, heat 1 tablespoon oil over moderately high heat until hot but not smoking.
2. Sauté mushrooms and half of onion, stirring, until mushrooms are tender and browned, 8 to 10 minutes.
3. Transfer to a bowl and wipe out skillet.
4. Peel and coarsely grate apple.
5. Stir into mushrooms with thyme, ½ teaspoon salt, and ¼ teaspoon pepper.
6. Preheat oven to 450 degrees F.
7. Peel potatoes and slice ⅛-inch thick preferably with a manual slicer.
8. Toss with remaining onion, salt, and pepper.
9. Heat remaining 2 tablespoons of oil in skillet over moderately high heat.
10. Add one third of potato slices in 1 layer, overlapping slightly.
11. Top with half of mushrooms, spreading in an even layer.
12. Repeat layering with half of remaining potatoes, remaining mushrooms, and then remaining potatoes.
13. Put skillet in middle of oven and bake 20 minutes.
14. Invert a pizza pan or round platter over skillet.
15. Holding pan or platter firmly against skillet, flip potato cake onto platter.
16. Carefully slide cake back into skillet.
17. Press layers together with a spatula.
18. Bake 8 to 10 minutes until underside is golden and crusty and potatoes are tender when pierced with a fork.
19. Transfer to serving plate.
20. Cut into wedges.
21. Serve immediately.

Onion Delights Cookbook

A Collection of Onion Recipes
Cookbook Delights Series-Book 8

Candies

Table of Contents

Page

Caramelized Onion Candy

I was surprised that so many young children liked this delicious candy.

Ingredients:

1 sweet onion, sliced
2 Tbs. butter
1 tsp. molasses
2 Tbs. brown sugar

Directions:

1. Place sliced onions on a large piece of aluminum foil.
2. Put butter on top, and sprinkle with brown sugar; drizzle with molasses.
3. Wrap up in foil; cook on grill until onions are caramelized.
4. Remove from grill, open foil to cool.
5. Scoop up candy with a spoon and enjoy.

Sweet Onion Truffles

These are truly unique! Try these savory, sweet chocolate candies.

Ingredients:

4 Tbs. butter
½ c. sweet onion, finely chopped
1¼ c. plus 2 Tbs. heavy cream
1 lb. plus 6 oz. milk chocolate, finely chopped
1 lb. semi-sweet dark covertures chocolate, finely chopped
2 c. Dutch process cocoa powder

Directions:

1. In a small heavy skillet, melt butter; add onion and sauté until golden brown.
2. Pour in heavy cream.
3. Let mixture come back to a boil; immediately remove from heat.
4. Strain cream mixture through a very fine strainer, pressing firmly to extract all juices, directly into bowl containing chopped milk chocolate.
5. Stir milk chocolate-cream mixture until chocolate is thoroughly melted.
6. Let chocolate truffle mixture stand at room temperature for 1 hour, until firm.
7. Scoop firm chocolate truffle mixture into tablespoon-size balls, rolling in your hands to round them.
8. Let scooped balls stand at cool room temperature for 30 minutes, until firm.
9. Gently melt semi-sweet chocolate until it is just about body temperature; a microwave at low power works well.
10. Transfer melted semi-sweet chocolate to medium bowl.
11. Wearing thin plastic gloves (for neatness), spoon small amount of melted dark chocolate into palm of your hand.
12. One at a time, roll chocolate truffle balls in between yours hands to coat them with thin film of dark chocolate.
13. Let chocolate coated truffles harden at cool room temperature, 5 to 10 minutes.
14. Have ready a shallow pan or bowl of Dutch cocoa.
15. When first layer of chocolate has set, repeat coating process of chocolate and then immediately roll in cocoa powder.
16. When firm, remove from cocoa powder, gently brush off excess cocoa, and transfer to serving tray.
17. Serve at room temperature.

Caramelized Onion Toffee Squares

This is a very unusual candy bar, but it is one that the children especially like with its crunchy texture and blended flavors. The onion causes the flavors to taste rich.

Ingredients:

1½ c. brown sugar, firmly packed
3 Tbs. corn syrup
½ c. sweet onion such as Vidalia, purе́ed
1 c. butter
1 c. sweet chocolate bits, melted
1 c. walnuts, chopped
1 c. coconut, lightly toasted in oven

Directions:

1. Lightly butter a 9 x 13-inch baking pan; sprinkle bottom with nuts; pour half of melted chocolate over nuts and place in freezer to harden well.
2. In skillet, over high heat, combine brown sugar, corn syrup, sweet onion, and butter.
3. Stir constantly until mixture begins to caramelize and thicken.
4. Cool a few minutes; do not let it harden in pan. Remove chocolate pan from freezer.
5. Pour caramelized mixture evenly over frozen chocolate.
6. Immediately pour the remaining melted chocolate over the top and sprinkle with toasted coconut.
7. Press coconut into chocolate as much as possible and then score into squares while still warm.
8. Place in refrigerator to cool completely.
9. Remove and break along scored lines; place on serving dish.
10. May be wrapped and stored in airtight container for up to one month.

Sweet Potato, Pecan, and Onion Candy

Try this unique combination of sweet potatoes and onions for a delicious treat!

Ingredients:

1 c. pecans, chopped
¼ c. sweet onions, very finely chopped
2 c. sugar
½ c. evaporated milk
¼ c. butter
½ tsp. vanilla extract
3 Tbs. marshmallow crème
½ c. sweet potatoes, cooked, mashed

Directions:

1. Lightly butter a baking sheet.
2. Scatter pecans on bottom of sheet; set aside.
3. In skillet, sauté onions until slightly browned; remove from heat and let cool.
4. In small saucepan, add sugar, milk, and butter.
5. Bring to boil and continue to boil for 2 to 3 minutes.
6. Cook until it starts to sugar; remove from heat.
7. Add vanilla and marshmallow crème.
8. Stir in sweet potatoes and sweet onions.
9. Beat until candy loses gloss.
10. Immediately pour over nuts on buttered baking sheet; cool.
11. Cut into squares.

Quotes . . . .

"And most, dear actors, eat no onions nor garlic, for we are to utter sweet breath.
-William Shakespeare (1564-1616) A Midsummer Night's Dream

Candied Jalapenos

These candied jalapenos are sweet, hot, and delicious.

Ingredients:

4 lb. fresh jalapeno peppers, sliced thin
2 lb. onions, diced
½ c. water
½ c. vinegar
6-8 c. sugar
2 Tbs. mustard seed
1 tsp. turmeric
2 tsp. celery seed (optional)
1 Tbs. garlic powder
1 tsp. ginger

Directions:

1. In large pot, place jalapenos and onions with water and vinegar.
2. Bring to a boil; reduce heat and simmer 10 minutes, or until tender, trying not to breathe the fumes.
3. Pour off most of the water-vinegar mixture.
4. Stir in sugar and spices.
5. Continue to simmer, to bring the mixture to soft candy temperature and to completely dissolve sugar, about 10 minutes.
6. Place boiling mixture into jars, leaving ¼-inch head-space.
7. Adjust caps.

"Banish (the onion) from the kitchen and the pleasure flies with it. Its presence lends color and enchantment to the most modest dish; its absence reduces the rarest delicacy to hopeless insipidity, and dinner to despair."
-Elizabeth Robbins Pennell, American columnist

Onion Delights Cookbook
A Collection of Onion Recipes
Cookbook Delights Series-Book 8

Cookies

Table of Contents

Fresh Apple Onion Cookies

These fragrant apple onion cookies make an excellent, healthy lunch treat, or leave them out for the children to have a late afternoon snack to hold them over until dinnertime.

Ingredients for cookies:

16 Tbs. butter
2⅔ c. brown sugar, firmly packed
2 eggs
2 tsp. baking soda
2 tsp. ground cloves
2 tsp. cinnamon
1 tsp. nutmeg
½ c. apple juice
4 c. flour
2 c. apples, chopped
½ c. sweet onions, finely chopped
2 c. raisins
2 c. nuts, chopped

Ingredients for glaze:

3 c. powdered sugar
5 Tbs. apple juice
1 tsp. vanilla extract
2 Tbs. butter

Directions for cookies:

1. Preheat oven to 375 degrees F.
2. Lightly grease baking sheets.
3. In large bowl, cream together butter, brown sugar, and eggs.
4. Add baking soda, spices, and juice; blend well.
5. Gradually add flour, mixing well after each addition.
6. Fold in apples, onions, raisins, and nuts of your choice.
7. Drop by heaping teaspoonfuls onto prepared baking sheets, 2 inches apart.
8. Bake 10 to 12 minutes, until lightly browned.

9. Remove from oven; transfer to wire rack and cool to lukewarm.

Directions for glaze:

1. While cookies are baking, in small bowl, combine powdered sugar, apple juice, and vanilla.
2. Beat in the butter until smooth and slightly thin.
3. With a knife, spread warm cookies with glaze.

Gingerbread Sweet Onion Cookies

These are always a delicious-tasting cookie and easy to make for the whole family.

Ingredients:

1⅓ c. brown sugar
⅓ c. butter
1 egg
5 tsp. vanilla extract
2¾ c. molasses
¾ c. sweet onions, finely chopped
5½ c. flour
4 tsp. baking soda
2 tsp. salt
5½ tsp. cinnamon
3 tsp. ginger

Directions:

1. In large bowl, cream together brown sugar and butter.
2. Add egg, vanilla, onion, and molasses; blend well.
3. In large bowl, sift flour, baking soda, salt, and spices together.
4. Add to the creamed mixture mixing well.
5. Cover and place in refrigerator to chill 2 hours.
6. Roll dough ¼-inch thick on a lightly floured surface; cut with a 2-inch cookie cutter.
7. Bake in preheated oven at 350 degrees F. for 8 to 10 minutes.
8. Remove from oven; place on wire rack to cool; decorate as desired before serving.

Orange Onion Cookie Bars

These cookie bars are quite delicious with the blends of flavor from the various ingredients. Your family and friends will enjoy your accomplishments in baking them.

Ingredients for bars:

¾ c. butter, softened
½ c. sugar
1 egg
1 tsp. vanilla extract
2 c. flour
2 tsp. baking powder
½ tsp. salt
½ tsp. ground nutmeg
½ c. orange juice
2 tsp. orange zest
½ c. coconut, flaked
1 c. carrots, cooked, mashed
½ c. sweet onions, chopped

Ingredients for glaze:

½ c. orange juice
1 tsp. orange zest
1½ c. powdered sugar

Directions for bars:

1. Preheat oven to 375 degrees F.
2. Lightly grease a 7 x 11-inch baking pan.
3. In medium bowl, cream together butter, sugar, egg, and vanilla until light and fluffy.
4. Sift together flour, baking powder, salt, and nutmeg.
5. Slowly add to creamed mixture, alternating with orange juice.
6. Fold in zest, coconut, onions, and carrots.
7. Spread batter into prepared baking pan.
8. Bake 40 minutes, or until inserted toothpick comes out clean.
9. Remove from oven and place cake, in pan, on wire rack to cool.

Directions for glaze:

1. In small bowl, combine orange juice, zest, and powdered sugar.
2. Warm slightly; pour over cooled bars in pan.
3. When ready to serve, cut into bars and remove from pan to serving dish.

Pletzl (Polish Onion Cookies)

These can be used as crackers as well. They will leave your mouth watering.

Ingredients:

1¼ c. butter, melted
¾ c. yogurt or buttermilk
3 c. flour
1 tsp. salt
1 egg, lightly beaten
2 lg. onions, minced
4 Tbs. poppy seeds
salt, to sprinkle on cookies

Directions:

1. In large mixing bowl, combine butter and yogurt.
2. Add flour, salt, egg, and onions; blend to make soft formed dough.
3. Cover and chill dough 1 hour in refrigerator.
4. Divide into two portions.
5. Roll out to ¼-inch thickness on a lightly floured surface.
6. Cut out with biscuit cutter.
7. Place on baking sheets; repeat with rest of dough.
8. Brush with lightly beaten egg and place ½ teaspoon of raw or sautéed onion on each.
9. Sprinkle with poppy seeds and small amount of salt.
10. Bake in preheated oven at 350 degrees F. for 12 to 15 minutes, or until light golden brown.
11. Remove from oven and place on wire rack to cool.

Natural Mountain Cookies

Made with many natural ingredients, these cookies are healthy as well as delicious.

Ingredients for cookies:

1 c. butter, soft
1 c. brown sugar
½ c. dark honey
½ c. molasses
½ c. sweet onions, finely chopped
½ c. dried berries, cherries, or cranberries
½ c. nuts, lightly chopped
3 c. flour
1 c. whole wheat flour
1 c. rolled oats
2 tsp. baking soda
3 tsp. ginger
½ c. cold, strong tea
1 tsp. vanilla extract
pinch of cloves

Ingredients for frosting:

1 c. powdered sugar
1½ Tbs. butter
½ tsp. lemon zest
½ tsp. almond extract
1½ Tbs. cream

Directions for cookies:

1. In large bowl, cream butter and sugar until light and fluffy.
2. Beat in molasses and honey.
3. Stir in onions, berries, and nuts.

4. In another bowl, combine flour, oats, baking soda, and spices.
5. Add dry ingredients alternately with tea and vanilla to creamed mixture; blend well.
6. Shape dough into a ball.
7. Wrap in wax paper and place in refrigerator for several hours.
8. Roll balls in palm of hand about walnut size.
9. Arrange on a baking sheet.
10. Press flat with fork dipped in flour.
11. Bake in preheated 375 degrees F. oven for 8 to 10 minutes.
12. Remove from oven and place on wire rack to cool.

Directions for frosting:

1. In small saucepan, melt butter.
2. Add powdered sugar, zest, almond extract, and cream.
3. Beat until well blended and smooth.
4. Decorate cooled cookies with frosting.
5. Replace on wire rack to set frosting.

Quotes . . . .

"Life is like an onion: You peel it off one layer at a time, and sometimes you weep."
-Carl Sandburg (1878-1967)

"My own remedy is always to eat, just before I step into bed, a hot roasted onion, if I have a cold."
-George Washington (attributed)

"An honest laborious country-man, with good bread, salt, and a little parsley, will make a contented meal with a roasted onion."
-John Evelyn (1620-1706)

Lemon Honey Specials with Sweet Onions

These truly are a melt-in-your-mouth cookie. The addition of the onion only increases the flavorful blends of honey and lemon.

Ingredients:

½ c. butter
½ c. brown sugar
½ c. honey
1 egg
1 tsp. lemon rind, grated
½ c. sweet onion, finely minced
2 c. flour, sifted
¼ tsp. salt
1 tsp. baking powder
1 c. wheat germ

Directions:

1. In large bowl, with an electric mixer, cream together butter, brown sugar, and honey until fluffy.
2. Add egg, minced onion, and lemon rind; beat well.
3. In small bowl, combine flour, salt, baking powder, and half of the wheat germ.
4. Mix into the creamed mixture.
5. Wrap dough in wax paper and refrigerate 1 hour.
6. Preheat oven to 350 degrees F.
7. Shape dough into 1-inch balls.
8. Roll the balls in the remaining wheat germ to coat.
9. Place on ungreased baking sheets 2 inches apart.
10. Flatten slightly with your finger or fork.
11. Bake 8 to 10 minutes, or until edges are light brown.
12. Remove with spatula and place on wire racks to cool.

13. Store in an airtight container for up to 1 month.

Onion Cookies (Laibele Kichel)

This is a traditional Jewish cookie, savory and full of flavor.

Ingredients:

- 6 c. flour
- 2 tsp. baking powder
- 2 tsp. salt
- ¾ c. poppy seeds
- 2 lg. onions, grated
- 3 eggs
- 1½ c. canola oil
- pepper, to taste

Directions:

1. Preheat oven to 400 degrees F.
2. Lightly grease baking sheets.
3. In large mixing bowl, sift together flour, baking powder, salt, and pepper to taste.
4. Add poppy seeds and mix briefly.
5. Make a well in center of dry ingredients.
6. Add eggs, grated onions, and oil, blending well. Dough will be stiff.
7. Let stand 10 minutes.
8. Divide dough into 4 pieces.
9. Roll out one piece at a time into medium-thin sheets.
10. Cut in desired size and shapes.
11. Continue until all of the dough is rolled and cut.
12. Place cookies onto prepared baking sheets.
13. Bake 10 to 12 minutes, or until very light brown.
14. Remove from oven; place on wire racks to cool.
15. Store in airtight containers.

Onion and Date Filled Cookies

The onions and dates make a very flavorful filling for these favorite cookies.

Ingredients:

1 c. dates, chopped
½ c. sweet onion, chopped
¼ c. walnuts or pecans, finely chopped
2½ c. flour
8 Tbs. butter
3 Tbs. water
1¼ c. brown sugar, divided
1 egg, beaten
pinch of salt
pinch of cinnamon

Ingredients for topping:

1½ c. honey
½ tsp. cinnamon
grated rind of ½ lemon

Directions:

1. Preheat oven to 350 degrees F.
2. Lightly grease a baking sheet.
3. In a covered colander, over boiling water, add dates and onions.
4. Steam 8 to 10 minutes until softened; cool and mash well.
5. Add nuts, ¼ cup of brown sugar, and a pinch of cinnamon; set aside.
6. In medium bowl, sift flour; cut in butter and combine well.
7. In separate bowl, combine water, egg, sugar, and salt; beat well.
8. Gradually add egg mixture to flour and butter mix; blend thoroughly.
9. Pinch off pieces of dough and roll into 1-inch balls.

10. Place on prepared baking sheet.
11. Depress center of each ball with your thumb.
12. Place 1 level teaspoon of date mixture in the depression.
13. Bake 20 minutes, or until lightly browned around date mixture.
14. Topping: In small bowl, mix honey, cinnamon, and grated lemon rind; drizzle over warm cookies.

Onion Sesame Seed Cookies

These are savory and tasty cookies. They have a cookie-like consistency, but they are not sweet.

Ingredients:

1 c. canola oil
¼ c. water
2 eggs
4 c. flour
1 tsp. baking soda
1 Tbs. salt
3 lg. onions, finely chopped
4 Tbs. sesame seeds

Directions:

1. Preheat oven to 400 degrees F.
2. Lightly grease baking sheets.
3. In medium bowl, combine oil, water, and eggs; beat well.
4. In large mixing bowl, sift together flour, baking soda, and salt; make a well in center.
5. Add beaten mixture and onions into center; mix into the flour slowly until stiff dough is obtained.
6. Divide dough into quarters and let set 15 minutes.
7. Roll very thin on floured surface.
8. Cut into rounds or squares; sprinkle each batch with the sesame seeds; press gently into top of cut-outs.
9. Place on prepared baking sheets; bake 10 to 15 minutes, or until golden brown. Cool on wire rack.

Orange Onion Marmalade Cookie Bars

Very moist and fruity, these bars are delicious with your coffee break anytime of the day.

Ingredients:

½ c. butter
½ c. sugar
½ tsp. almond extract
½ tsp. vanilla extract
1 egg
1½ c. flour
1 tsp. baking powder
½ tsp. ground cinnamon
¼ tsp. ground cloves
½ tsp. salt
½ c. orange marmalade
½ c. onion jam, or brown sugar caramelized onions

Directions:

1. Preheat oven to 400 degrees F.
2. Lightly grease an 8-inch baking pan.
3. In large mixing bowl, cream butter with sugar and extracts.
4. Beat in egg; blend well.
5. In separate bowl, sift together flour, baking powder, cinnamon, cloves, and salt.
6. Combine dry ingredients with creamed mixture; beat until smooth.
7. Spread half of the dough into prepared baking pan.
8. Cover evenly with the combined marmalade and onion jam.
9. Spread the remaining dough over the top.
10. Bake 25 minutes.
11. Cool on wire rack.
12. Cut into bars.

Onion Chocolate Chip Cookies

The onions look similar to coconut sprinkles, but of course with a very different flavor. Surprise your guests with these savory, succulent cookies.

Ingredients:

- 2½ c. flour
- 1 tsp. baking soda
- 1 tsp. salt
- 1 c. butter, softened
- ¾ c. brown sugar
- ¾ c. sugar
- 2 eggs
- 1 tsp. vanilla extract
- 1 pkg. chocolate chips (12 oz.)
- 1 med. Vidalia onion, chopped

Directions:

1. Preheat oven to 375 degrees F.
2. Lightly grease baking sheets.
3. In medium bowl, combine flour, baking soda, and salt; set aside.
4. In large bowl, beat together butter, sugar, and brown sugar until creamy and light.
5. Beat in eggs one at a time; add vanilla.
6. Add flour in two additions, mixing well.
7. Stir in chocolate chips.
8. Remove moisture from onions by pressing between paper towels; reserve.
9. Spoon cookie dough by heaping teaspoonfuls 2 inches apart onto prepared baking sheets.
10. Flatten with wet fingers and sprinkle reserved onions on top of each cookie; press in slightly.
11. Bake 12 to 14 minutes, or until golden brown.
12. Remove from oven and lift to wire rack to cool.

Peanut Butter and Onion Cookies

This is a really tasty cookie with a soft texture from the addition of onions. Make a large batch, as everyone will love these.

Ingredients:

½ c. butter
1¼ c. light brown sugar
¾ c. peanut butter
1 egg
3 Tbs. milk
¼ c. onions, puréed
1 Tbs. vanilla extract
2 c. flour
¾ tsp. baking soda
¾ tsp. salt

Directions:

1. Preheat oven to 375 degrees F.
2. In medium bowl, cream together butter, brown sugar, and peanut butter until smooth.
3. Stir in egg, milk, onion, and vanilla.
4. In small bowl, combine flour, baking soda, and salt.
5. Stir into peanut butter mixture; blend well.
6. Drop by rounded spoonfuls onto an ungreased baking sheet.
7. Bake 12 to 15 minutes.
8. Allow cookies to cool on baking sheet for 3 minutes.
9. Removing to a wire rack to cool completely.
10. Store in airtight container.

Yields: 4 dozen cookies.

Raisin Onion Cookie Bars

These cookie squares are definitely a delicious treat to serve to family or guests. The combination of onions with the raisins adds more flavor to an already tasty cookie.

Ingredients for crust:

½ c. brown sugar
½ c. butter
½ c. flour
¾ c. rolled oats

Ingredients for filling:

2 eggs
1 c. brown sugar
1 tsp. vanilla extract
½ c. flour
¼ tsp. salt
½ tsp. baking powder
¾ c. raisins
½ c. sweet onion, chopped
½ c. coconut, flaked
½ c. pitted sour cherries, drained with liquid reserved

Directions for crust:

1. Preheat oven to 350 degrees F.
2. In medium bowl, mix together brown sugar, butter, flour, and oats until crumbly.
3. Press into the bottom of a 9-inch square pan.
4. Bake for 15 minutes.
5. Remove from oven and set aside.

Directions for filling:

1. In medium bowl, cream together eggs, brown sugar, and vanilla.
2. Stir in flour, salt, and baking powder until well blended.

3. Fold in raisins, onions, coconut, and cherries, adding a little bit of the cherry juice if needed to keep batter from becoming to stiff.
4. Spread over baked crust.
5. Return to oven for 30 minutes, or until firm and lightly browned.
6. Cool to lukewarm in pan; cut into bars.

Sweet Onion Cookies

These are surprisingly sweet and flavorful. Your family and guests will be impressed.

Ingredients:

1 c. sweet onions, chopped
½ c. butter
1 c. sugar
1 c. cooked squash
1 tsp. vanilla extract
2 c. flour
1 tsp. baking powder
1 tsp. baking soda
½ tsp. salt
1 Tbs. cinnamon

Directions:

1. Preheat oven to 375 degrees F.
2. Lightly grease a baking sheet.
3. In small saucepan, cook onions in small amount of water until tender.
4. In large mixing bowl, cream together butter, sugar, onions, and squash; add vanilla.
5. In medium bowl, sift together flour, baking powder, baking soda, salt, and cinnamon; add to cream mixture and blend well.
6. Drop from teaspoon onto prepared baking sheet.
7. Bake 12 to 15 minutes.
8. Remove from oven; lift with spatula to wire rack to cool.

Desserts

Table of Contents

Page

Caramelized Sweet Onion and Apple Pizza

This is such a delicious dessert that you may want to make more than one.

Ingredients for crust:

½ c. butter, softened
¼ c. powdered sugar
1 c. flour, sifted

Ingredients for topping:

½ c. sweet onions, diced
1 c. brown sugar, firmly packed, divided
¼ c. water
2 c. fresh apples, sliced
1 c. Cheddar cheese, shredded
½ tsp. ground cinnamon

Directions for crust:

1. Preheat oven to 350 degrees F.
2. In medium bowl, cream together butter and powdered sugar.
3. Add flour; mix gently just until dough comes together; pat evenly into a 12-inch pizza pan.
4. Bake 15 minutes.
5. Remove from oven and set aside for topping.

Directions for topping:

1. In skillet, over medium heat, place onion, ½ cup brown sugar, and water.
2. Cook until onions become translucent; add apple slices and stir gently for 2 minutes.
3. Cool mixture and then spread over top of baked dough.

4. In medium bowl, mix together cheese, remainder of brown sugar, and cinnamon. Sprinkle over the onion and apple topping.
5. Return pizza to oven for 25 to 30 minutes longer.
6. Remove from oven; place on wire rack to cool.
7. When ready to serve, slice in small wedges.

Onion Crumb Pudding with Pineapple

This pineapple bread pudding becomes even more delicious with the addition of sweet onions to boost the flavor.

Ingredients:

1 c. pineapple tidbits
1 c. sweet onion, diced
3 eggs, beaten
⅓ c. mandarin oranges, crushed
3 Tbs. flour
½ c. nonfat milk
2 Tbs. honey
1 Tbs. brown sugar
1 tsp. ground cinnamon
½ tsp. ground nutmeg
½ tsp. ground cloves
4 c. dry bread crumbs
½ c. raisins

Directions:

1. Preheat oven to 350 degrees F.
2. Lightly grease a baking dish.
3. In large bowl, combine onion, pineapple, eggs, oranges, flour, milk, and honey to form a batter.
4. Stir in brown sugar, cinnamon, nutmeg, and cloves.
5. Fold in bread crumbs and raisins.
6. Spoon into prepared dish.
7. Bake 30 minutes, until set.
8. Remove from oven; place on wire rack to cool.

Sweet Onion Pecan Delight

This pecan crust sets this onion and chocolate dessert above the ordinary.

Ingredients for crust:

¼ c. sweet onion, finely chopped
¼ c. brown sugar
1 c. flour
½ c. butter
1 c. pecans, finely chopped

Ingredients for filling:

1 pkg. cream cheese (8 oz.)
1 c. powdered sugar
3 c. frozen whipped topping, thawed
1 pkg. instant chocolate pudding mix
1 pkg. instant vanilla pudding mix
3 c. milk
2 Tbs. pecans, chopped

Directions for crust:

1. Preheat oven to 350 degrees F.
2. Lightly butter a 9 x 13-inch glass baking dish.
3. Place chopped onions onto paper towels.
4. Blot excess moisture; onions should be almost dry.
5. Spread thin layer of onions on plate.
6. Sprinkle brown sugar over top; set aside.
7. In medium bowl, cut butter into the flour with a pastry blender or two knives, until mixture resembles coarse meal.
8. Stir in pecans and onions sprinkled with the brown sugar.
9. Mix until well blended.
10. Place in prepared baking dish.

11. Press mixture onto bottom and 1 inch up sides.
12. Bake 15 minutes, or until golden brown.
13. Remove from oven.
14. Place on wire rack to cool completely.

Directions for filling:

1. In medium bowl, combine cream cheese, powdered sugar, and 1 cup of whipped topping.
2. Beat with electric mixer until smooth.
3. In separate bowl, whisk together both pudding mixes with the milk until smooth.
4. Combine with cream cheese mixture.
5. Whisk until smooth.
6. Pour into cooled crust.
7. Spread remaining whipped topping over the pudding mixture.
8. Sprinkle 2 tablespoons of chopped nuts on top.
9. Chill in refrigerator until ready to serve.

Did You Know? . . . .

Did you know that you can mix hot chamomile tea with onion juice to lighten your hair?

Quotes . . . .

"Red onions are especially divine. I hold a slice up to the sunlight pouring in through the kitchen window, and it glows like a fine piece of antique glass. Cool watery-white with layers delicately edged with imperial purple...strong, humble, peaceful...with that fiery nub of spring green in the center..."
-Mary Hayes Grieco, "The Kitchen Mystic"

Sweet Onion Custard with Corn Ice Cream

This is certainly an unusual dessert, but it is actually quite good, though it is only mildly sweet.

Ingredients for custard:

- 3 sweet onions, finely chopped
- 4 Tbs. olive oil
- 2 green tomatoes, chopped
- 2 garlic cloves
- 1 bunch Italian parsley, finely chopped
- 10 eggs
- 1 qt. heavy cream
- salt and pepper, to taste
- hot sauce

Ingredients for corn ice cream:

- 1 c. milk
- ½ c. heavy cream
- ½ c. corn, roasted
- 4 egg yolks
- 4 Tbs. sugar

Directions for custard:

1. Preheat oven to 325 degrees F.
2. Lightly butter a casserole dish or individual custard dishes.
3. In skillet, over medium heat, sauté onion until transparent; avoid browning.
4. Add green tomatoes, garlic, parsley, hot sauce, and salt and pepper to taste; set aside.
5. In medium bowl, whisk 10 whole eggs until foamy.
6. In small saucepan, bring heavy cream to a boil.
7. Remove from heat and cool to lukewarm.

8. Pour some cream into whipped eggs; blend well.
9. Combine egg mixture back into the cream.
10. Add mixture to the onion mixture.
11. Pour into prepared dish.
12. If desired to avoid outside browning, place in water bath containers while baking or use crock type containers.
13. Bake 45 minutes, or until knife inserted in center comes out clean.

Directions for corn ice cream:

1. In large saucepan, mix kernel corn, milk, and heavy cream together.
2. Bring to boil.
3. Simmer 10 minutes.
4. Cool only enough to handle and place in a blender.
5. Blend until smooth; strain through a sieve.
6. Whisk eggs and sugar until foamy.
7. Mix one third of the eggs into cream.
8. Add egg mixture back to remainder of cream.
9. Set aside; cool completely.
10. Place in ice cream maker and follow manufacturer's instructions.
11. When done place in freezer until ready to serve.
12. Scoop over top of custard.

Quotes . . . .

"Happy is said to be the family which can eat onions together. They are, for the time being, separate, from the world, and have a harmony of aspiration."
-Charles Dudley Warner, My Summer in a Garden (1871)

"onions do promote a man to veneryous actes, and to somnolence."
-Andrew Boorde (1542) "Dietary of Helthe"

Vidalia Sweet Onion and Peach Bake

With the sweet onion bringing out the flavors of this delicious dessert itself, add some French vanilla ice cream and make it a dream come true.

Ingredients for bake:

¼ c. butter
1 c. light brown sugar, firmly packed
1 med. Vidalia onion, thinly sliced
1 c. white rice, uncooked
½ c. pecans, chopped
2 sm. pieces gingerroot, thinly sliced
1 c. fresh peaches, sliced
½ fresh lemon, grated zest, juiced
½ c. fresh sweet cherries, chopped
¼ tsp. salt
4 c. peach or apricot nectar
1 Tbs. cornstarch

Ingredients for topping:

¼ c. butter
1 c. brown sugar
¾ c. orange juice
½ fresh lemon, juiced and grated zest
1 Tbs. cornstarch
pecans, chopped

Directions for bake:

1. Preheat oven to 350 degrees F.
2. Lightly butter a 2-quart casserole dish.
3. In skillet, over medium heat, melt butter and brown sugar. Stir in onion, rice, and pecans.
4. Cook and stir until rice is lightly browned.

5. Mix in ginger, peaches with lemon juice, and zest; add cherries and stir 3 minutes.
6. Stir in salt, nectar, and cornstarch.
7. Transfer mixture to prepared dish.
8. Bake 1 hour, or until liquid has been absorbed and rice is tender.
9. Add more liquid without stirring if rice is not completely cooked; leave an additional 15 to 20 minutes to finish.
10. Remove from oven and place on wire rack to cool, then chill in refrigerator until ready to serve.

Directions for topping:

1. In small saucepan, place brown sugar, butter, and orange juice; bring to boil.
2. Add lemon juice, zest, and cornstarch; cook down until lightly thickened.
3. Remove from heat and cool.
4. Spoon over the bake, sprinkle with pecans and serve with ice cream along side.

Quotes . . . .

"Onions can make even heirs and widows weep."
-Benjamin Franklin

"The kitchen, reasonably enough, was the scene of my first gastronomic adventure. I was on all fours. I crawled into the vegetable bin, settled on a giant onion and ate it, skin and all. It must have marked me for life, for I have never ceased to love the hearty flavor of raw onions."
-James Beard (1903-1985)

"I understand the big food companies are developing a tearless onion. I think they can do it – after all, they've already given us tasteless bread."
-Robert Orben (1927)

Walla Walla Sweet Ricotta Cheesecake

This is a unique, savory cheesecake with a sweet onion and mint topping. The ricotta cheese needs to be drained overnight, as in directions.

Ingredients for crust:

3 c. graham crackers, finely ground
½ c. butter, melted

Ingredients for onion filling:

2 lg. Walla Walla sweet onions, peeled, chopped
1½ Tbs. butter
1 qt. heavy cream
½ tsp. ground cinnamon
2 c. Arborio or sushi rice

Ingredients for ricotta filling:

1 lb. ricotta cheese, drained (see directions)
1 c. sugar
8 eggs
3 lb. cream cheese
2½ c. onion filling (see above)

Ingredients for topping:

1 Tbs. butter
2 Tbs. sugar
2 med. Walla Walla sweet onions, peeled, grated
3 Tbs. honey
½ c. fresh mint, chopped

Directions for crust:

1. In large bowl, thoroughly combine graham crackers and butter to crumbly texture.

2. Press into bottom and 2 inches up sides of a round 10 x 3-inch springform pan.
3. Cover and refrigerate until ready to use.

Directions for onion filling:

1. In large saucepan, over low heat, sauté onions in butter until liquid has been released, and onions are translucent; avoid browning.
2. Add cream, cinnamon, and rice.
3. Cook over low heat until rice is cooked and onions disintegrate in form.
4. Remove from heat.
5. Cool completely.
6. Place in blender or food processor.
7. Purée until smooth and set aside.

Directions for ricotta filling:

1. The night before you want to bake the cake, line a medium bowl with cheesecloth.
2. Fill cloth with ricotta cheese.
3. Set plate atop cheese to weigh it down.
4. Let sit overnight.
5. The following day, wrap ricotta cheese in cheesecloth.
6. Wring out as much liquid as possible.
7. Transfer cheese to fine mesh sieve.
8. Using plastic spatula, force cheese through and into large stainless steel bowl.
9. Preheat oven to 300 degrees F.
10. Combine the ricotta with eggs, sugar, cream cheese, and onion filling.
11. Pour ricotta filling into prepared crust.
12. Place pan into larger, high-sided roasting pan and carefully pour boiling water into roasting pan around springform pan to depth of 1½ inches; this will reduce cracking on top of cheesecake.

13. Bake 40 to 45 minutes, or until middle of cheesecake is nearly set when shaken and slightly puffy.
14. Remove from oven.
15. Cool on wire rack.
16. Refrigerate until ready to serve.

Directions for topping:

1. In small saucepan, over low heat, cook butter with sugar until golden brown.
2. Add onions and toss to combine.
3. Sauté until onions are light brown.
4. Add enough honey, just until onions are coated and bound together. You may need to use more or less than 3 tablespoons, depending on the amount of liquid in onions.
5. Remove mixture from heat; cool.
6. Gently fold in mint until well incorporated.
7. Cut cheesecake into wedge-shaped slices.
8. Place 1 tablespoon of topping on wide end of each slice for garnish.

Quotes . . . .

"There are two types of onions, the big white Spanish and the little red Italian. The Spanish has more food value and is therefore chosen to make soup for the huntsmen and drunkards, two classes of people who require fast recuperation."
-Alexandre Dumas (1802-1870)

"Beet ever so onion there snow peas legume."
-Margaret Thornley, in "A Kick in the Seat of the Pants" Roger von Oech

Onion Delights Cookbook
A Collection of Onion Recipes
Cookbook Delights Series-Book 8

Dressings, Sauces, and Condiments

Table of Contents

Page

Avocado Onion Dressing

This is an excellent, tangy dressing that is great for use on a tossed green salad. Try it over romaine lettuce with cooked shrimp and tomato wedges.

Ingredients:

1 lg. avocado, pitted, peeled
2 Tbs. lemon juice
1 c. mayonnaise
½ c. sour cream
½ tsp. hot sauce
⅓ c. onion, chopped
2 garlic cloves, minced
1 tsp. salt
1 dash cayenne pepper

Directions:

1. In small bowl, mash avocado with lemon juice.
2. In blender, add mayonnaise, sour cream, and hot sauce; blend lightly.
3. Add onion and garlic.
4. Adjust salt and pepper to taste; blend until smooth.
5. Cover; chill until ready to serve.

Balsamic Vinaigrette with Shallots

This balsamic vinaigrette is delicious and simple to make. The shallots give it a unique flavor.

Ingredients:

¾ c. olive oil
¼ c. balsamic vinegar
1 shallot, finely chopped

¼ tsp. salt
¼ tsp. pepper, freshly ground

Directions:

1. Combine oil and vinegar in shaker jar to break up the oil.
2. Add shallot, salt, and pepper.
3. Close tightly; shake vigorously.
4. Place in refrigerator until ready to serve over salad.

Blue Cheese and Onion Dressing

This is one of my all-time favorite dressings. It has a savory, complex flavor and complements any salad you are serving.

Ingredients:

⅓ lb. blue cheese, crumbled lightly
½ c. sour cream
½ c. buttermilk
1 c. mayonnaise
¼ tsp. garlic salt
1 tsp. fresh onion, minced
1 tsp. dried onion
salt and pepper, to taste

Directions:

1. In medium bowl, place cheese, sour cream, buttermilk, and mayonnaise together; blend well.
2. Add garlic, fresh and dried onion, and salt and pepper to taste.
3. Cover.
4. Chill in refrigerator until ready to serve.

Creamy Pesto Sauce

Quick and easy pesto is a great change from red sauce over your favorite pasta. My family really enjoys this tasty pesto sauce.

Ingredients:

3 c. fresh basil leaves
1½ c. walnuts, chopped
4 garlic cloves, peeled
⅓ c. Parmesan cheese, freshly grated
1 c. olive oil
salt and pepper, to taste

Directions:

1. In food processor, blend together basil leaves, nuts, garlic, and cheese.
2. Set blender to low speed and pour in oil slowly while still mixing.
3. Stir in salt and pepper to taste.
4. Cover and store in refrigerator until ready to serve.

Yields: 2 cups.

Creamy Vinaigrette

Creamy vinaigrette is a nice alternative to the heavier cream versions and can be achieved by using rice wine vinegar and mayonnaise.

Ingredients:

¼ c. rice wine vinegar
2 Tbs. mayonnaise
1 lg. garlic clove, minced
⅔ c. olive oil

1 Tbs. onion, finely chopped
salt and black pepper, to taste

Directions:

1. In small skillet, sauté onions with butter until transparent, about 3 minutes; remove from heat.
2. Measure vinegar and mayonnaise into 2-cup measuring cup.
3. With small whisk, stir in garlic, onion, salt and pepper to taste.
4. Measure oil in another cup; with continuous whisking, add oil slowly in droplets, then in a slow steady stream to make emulsified vinaigrette.
5. Cover and chill in refrigerator until ready to serve.

Gorgonzola and Onion Dressing

Gorgonzola cheese adds a unique flavor to this delicious dressing.

Ingredients:

1 Tbs. onion, finely chopped
6 oz. olive oil
2 oz. sherry or wine vinegar
2 oz. soft Gorgonzola cheese
salt and pepper, to taste

Directions:

1. In skillet, over medium heat, sauté onion until transparent, remove from heat.
2. Cream together oil, vinegar, and cheese.
3. Combine and blend with the onions; add salt and pepper to taste.
4. Cover and refrigerate until ready to serve over salad.

Herbed Onion Butter

The herbs and green onions add flavor to this herbed butter. It is especially tasty on fresh corn on the cob.

Ingredients:

½ c. butter, softened
3 Tbs. fresh Italian parsley, chopped
1 Tbs. fresh oregano, chopped
1 green onion, finely chopped
1 Tbs. fresh chives, chopped
1 Tbs. fresh basil, chopped

Directions:

1. In small bowl, combine butter, parsley, oregano, green onion, chives, and basil.
2. Blend well by mashing together to release and mingle flavors.
3. Scrape mixture onto the center of a 12-inch length piece of plastic wrap.
4. Fold over one side and shape butter into a roll.
5. Twist ends to seal; refrigerate until ready to use.
6. Note: This may be kept in the refrigerator tightly wrapped for several weeks.

Huckleberry Onion Vinaigrette

Huckleberry vinegar and onions make a great salad dressing flavor. Try it as a creamy dressing by adding your choice of mayonnaise, yogurt, or sour cream.

Ingredients:

½ c. olive oil
6 Tbs. huckleberry balsamic vinegar
1 tsp. dried onion

1 tsp. salt
¼ tsp. black pepper, ground
mayonnaise, yogurt, or sour cream (optional)

Directions:

1. In shaker jar or bowl, combine the oil and vinegar.
2. Shake or whisk to break up oil.
3. Add onion, and salt and pepper to taste.
4. For creamier dressing, stir in 1 tablespoon mayonnaise, plain yogurt, or sour cream.
5. Cover; refrigerate until ready to serve.

Minced Onion French Dressing

Onions add zest to this classic and well-loved French dressing.

Ingredients:

2 c. canola oil
1 Tbs. onion, minced
¼ tsp. garlic powder
1 tsp. paprika
⅛ tsp. black pepper
½ tsp. dry mustard
1½ tsp. salt
1 Tbs. sugar
¾ c. cider vinegar

Directions:

1. In small bowl, combine oil, onion, garlic powder, paprika, pepper, mustard, salt, and sugar.
2. Let stand for at least 1 hour to bring out flavors.
3. Add cider vinegar.
4. Beat or whisk to blend well.
5. Store in refrigerator until ready to use.

Onion Vinaigrette

This is a very flavorful vinaigrette and simple to make. Use over your favorite salad.

Ingredients:

1 c. canola oil
½ c. vinegar
1 c. sugar
1 tsp. salt
1 tsp. dry mustard
1 tsp. celery seed
1 med. onion, finely chopped
2 Tbs. water, hot

Directions:

1. In blender, combine oil and vinegar to break up oil.
2. Add sugar, salt, mustard celery seed, onion, and water; blend until smooth.
3. Pour into covered container and refrigerate until ready to serve.

Poppy Seed Dressing

Dijon mustard and poppy seeds add a fine flavor and interesting texture to this dressing.

Ingredients:

¾ c. sugar
¾ Tbs. Dijon mustard
⅛ tsp. salt
¼ red onion, finely chopped
⅔ c. red wine vinegar
2 c. canola oil
4 Tbs. poppy seeds

Directions:

1. In blender, combine sugar, mustard, salt, onion, and red wine vinegar; blend until smooth.
2. Add oil and blend again to break up oil.
3. Pulsate two times to whisk in poppy seeds.
4. Pour into covered container and refrigerate until ready to serve.

Ranch Dressing with Green Onions

The cottage cheese adds pizzazz to this traditional ranch dressing.

Ingredients:

2 c. cottage cheese
½ c. yogurt, drained
2 sm. garlic cloves, minced
1 tsp. dried oregano
1 tsp. dried thyme
½ c. green onions, finely chopped
2 tsp. fresh parsley, chopped
½ c. buttermilk
2 Tbs. lemon juice
1 Tbs. red wine vinegar
white pepper, freshly ground, to taste

Directions:

1. In blender, combine cheese, yogurt, garlic, spices, green onion, and parsley; purée.
2. Add buttermilk, lemon juice, vinegar, and pepper to taste; blend until creamy and smooth.
3. Pour into covered container and refrigerate until ready to serve.

Yields: 8 servings.

Russian Dressing

Try this Russian dressing for a zingy, delicious new taste for a favorite salad dressing.

Ingredients:

1 c. mayonnaise
¼ c. ketchup
1 Tbs. horseradish
1 tsp. onion, grated

Directions:

1. In small bowl, combine mayonnaise, ketchup, horseradish, and grated onion.
2. Whisk together until well blended.
3. Place in covered container.
4. Store in refrigerator until ready to serve.

Thousand Island Dressing

Try this homemade version of the traditional Thousand Island dressing.

Ingredients:

½ c. mayonnaise
2 Tbs. ketchup
1 Tbs. white vinegar
2 tsp. sugar
2 tsp. dill pickle relish
1 tsp. white onion, finely minced
⅛ tsp. salt
dash of black pepper

Directions:

1. In small bowl, combine mayonnaise, ketchup, vinegar, and sugar; blend well.
2. Add relish, onion, and salt and pepper to taste, stirring well.
3. Place in covered container; refrigerate for several hours, stirring occasionally, so sugar dissolves and flavors blend.
4. Keep refrigerated until ready to serve.

Onion Pesto Sauce

I love pine nuts, and this delicious pesto sauce is almost addictive!

Ingredients:

⅓ c. pine nuts, toasted
1 bunch parsley, rinsed
1 bunch fresh basil or 3 Tbs. dried basil
¼ c. Parmesan cheese
1 lg. onion, peeled, chopped
½ c. olive oil
salt and pepper, to taste

Directions:

1. Preheat oven to 350 degrees F.
2. Toast pine nuts on a baking sheet, watching carefully that they do not get too dark; set aside.
3. Remove stems from parsley and basil.
4. Place cheese, onion, nuts, parsley, and basil in food processor.
5. Process 30 seconds, or until finely chopped.
6. With blender on low, add olive oil in a slow steady stream until mixture reaches desired thickness.
7. Pour into a container and cover.
8. Refrigerate until ready to serve.

Classic Ranch Mix Dip and Dressing

This mix is similar to the bought variety, but much more satisfying when you make your own to pull from the shelves when you need it. Stored in a jar, it can even double for a really great gift.

Ingredients:

15 saltines
2 c. dry parsley flakes, minced
½ c. instant minced onion
2 Tbs. dry dill weed
¼ c. onion powder
¼ c. onion salt
¼ c. garlic powder
¼ c. garlic salt
buttermilk
mayonnaise
sour cream

Directions:

1. Place crackers in blender container; blend on high speed until powdered.
2. Add parsley, minced onion, and dill weed.
3. Blend again until powdered.
4. Place in medium mixing bowl.
5. Stir in onion powder and salt, garlic powder and salt.
6. Place into a lidded airtight container.
7. Store dry mix at room temperature for up to a year.

To reconstitute mix:

1. Combine 1 tablespoon dry mix with 1 cup mayonnaise and 1 cup buttermilk.

Onion Delights Cookbook
A Collection of Onion Recipes
Cookbook Delights Series-Book 8

Jams, Jellies, and Syrups

Table of Contents

A Basic Guide for Canning Jams, Jellies, and Syrups

1. Wash jars in hot, soapy water inside and out with brush or soft cloth.
2. Run your finger around rim of each jar, discarding any with cracks or chips.
3. Rinse well in clean, clear, hot water, using tongs to avoid burns to hands or fingers.
4. Place upside down on clean cloth to drain well.
5. Place lids in boiling water for 2 minutes to sterilize and keep hot until placing on rim of jar.
6. Immediately prior to filling each jar, immerse in very hot water with tongs to heat jar (avoids breakage of jar with hot liquid).
7. Fill jar to within 1 inch of top of rim or to level recommended in recipe.
8. Wipe rim with clean damp cloth to remove any particles of food, and check again for any chips or cracks.
9. With tongs, place lid from hot bath directly onto rim of jar.
10. Using gloves, cloth, or holders, tighten lid firmly onto jar with ring or use single formed lid in place of ring to cover inner lid. Do not tighten down too hard as it may impede sealing.
11. Place on protected surface to cool, taking care to not disturb lid and ring. A slight indentation of lid will be apparent when sealed.
12. Leave overnight until thoroughly cooled.
13. When cooled, wipe jars with damp cloth and then label and date each.
14. Store upright on shelf in cool, dark place.

Quotes . . . .

"Life is like an onion; you peel off layer after layer and then you find there is nothing in it."
-James Gibbons Huneker, American musician, critic

Caramelized Onion Jam

Caramelized onion jam makes a great gift because it is so unusual. It is a great accompaniment to your main course. This versatile jam can be made in the traditional way and stored in a jar, or it may also be stored in the freezer.

Ingredients:

- 3 Tbs. butter
- 4 lg. onions, sliced
- ⅔ c. brown sugar, firmly packed
- ½ c. brown malt vinegar
- 1 tsp. fresh rosemary, finely chopped

Directions:

1. In large pan, heat butter; add onions and cook gently 20 to 30 minutes, until onions are very soft and lightly browned.
2. Add sugar; stir until melted.
3. Simmer uncovered, stirring occasionally, until mixture is thick and caramelized.
4. Add vinegar and simmer uncovered for an additional 5 minutes until thickened slightly.
5. Remove from heat and stir in the rosemary.
6. Process following a basic guide for canning found in the front of this section.
7. After opening or thawing, may be refrigerated for 2 to 3 weeks.

Did You Know? . . . .

Did you know that you could place a slice of onion on the affected area of skin to relieve insect bites, stinging nettle rashes, and hives?

Delicious Onion Jam

This onion jam is particularly savory and delicious. Try some over chicken or beef as well as pork.

Ingredients:

- 8 c. red onions, thinly sliced
- 1½ c. apple juice
- ½ c. wine vinegar
- 4 tsp. fresh sage, chopped
- ½ tsp. ground dried sage
- 3 tsp. ground black pepper
- 4 c. sugar
- 1 pkg. low sugar pectin
- ½ c. brown sugar, packed
- ½ tsp. butter

Directions:

1. In large pot, combine onions, apple juice, vinegar, and spices.
2. Mix ¼ cup of the sugar with the pectin.
3. Add to the onion mixture.
4. Add butter and bring to a full boil; stir constantly.
5. Add remaining sugar and boil 5 minutes longer.
6. Ladle into prepared jars.
7. Process following a basic guide for canning found in the front of this section.

Yields: 7 cups.

Did You Know? . . . .

Did you know that the thickness of an onion skin can help predict the severity of the winter? According to an old English rhyme, thin skins mean a mild winter is coming while thick skins indicate a rough winter ahead.

Onion Jam

Try this "jam" with the rich flavor of balsamic vinegar and onions, on your favorite sandwich.

Ingredients:

¼ lb. butter
8 lb. yellow onions, peeled, cut into chunks
¼ c. light honey
¼ c. balsamic vinegar

Directions:

1. Place onions in a food processor; coarsely chop.
2. In an 8-quart pot, place butter and onions.
3. Cover and sauté over medium heat, stirring occasionally to avoid scorching.
4. When onions have cooked down to half their original volume, reduce heat to low and continue cooking until onions are a caramel color.
5. Remove cover; add honey and vinegar.
6. Continue cooking until onions become mushy and thickened with juice absorbed.
7. Check flavor; there should be no sharp onion taste; add more honey if necessary.
8. Process following a basic guide for canning found in the front of this section.
9. After opening, onion jam can be refrigerated, covered, for 2 to 3 weeks.

Did You Know? . . . .

Did you know that you can keep your windshield from frosting at night? Slice an onion and rub the windshield with the onion. The juice will keep it frost-free.

Sweet Onion Jelly

This onion jelly is great with beef, chicken, or pork. Try using this on your favorite meat sandwich.

Ingredients:

3 c. sweet onions, chopped
¾ c. cider vinegar
3 c. sugar
1 tsp. red pepper flakes, crushed
1 pkg. powdered fruit pectin

Directions:

1. In blender, purée onion and vinegar in until smooth.
2. Pour into saucepan.
3. Over medium heat, add sugar and crushed pepper flakes; bring to a boil.
4. Boil 5 minutes; add powdered pectin; stir to combine.
5. Bring to a hard boil; boil for 1 minute.
6. Process following a basic guide for canning found in the front of this section.

Sweet Onion Preserves

These preserves are great as an accompaniment to your meat or main dish, and they are a nice addition to your holiday feast.

Ingredients:

½ c. extra virgin olive oil
3 lb. sweet onions, peeled, thinly sliced
¾ c. light brown sugar, packed
⅔ c. tarragon white wine vinegar
1 c. dry white wine
¼ c. fresh tarragon leaves, minced
1 tsp. white pepper, freshly ground

Directions:

1. Heat oil in nonstick pan over medium heat.
2. Stir in onions and sugar; reduce heat to low.
3. Cover and cook, stirring occasionally for 30 minutes.
4. Add vinegar and wine; cook, uncovered, over medium-low heat, stirring occasionally, for 45 minutes, or until mixture is thick.
5. Remove from heat; stir in tarragon and pepper.
6. Process following a basic guide for canning found in the front of this section.

Walla Walla Onion Jam

Walla Walla onions are sweet and full of flavor. Enjoy this full-flavored onion jam.

Ingredients:

2 Tbs. olive oil
2 lg. Walla Walla onions, peeled, thinly sliced
2 Tbs. brown sugar
2 Tbs. rice vinegar
3 Tbs. golden raisins, chopped
salt and pepper, to taste

Directions:

1. In large skillet, over medium heat, heat olive oil.
2. Add onions, cooking and stirring just until turning color.
3. Add sugar; continue cooking, 15 to 20 minutes, until onions are golden brown and very soft.
4. If onions appear to be browning too quickly, add 1 tablespoon water.
5. Stir in vinegar and raisins; season to taste with salt and pepper.
6. Cool; cover and refrigerate for up to 3 weeks, or process following a basic guide for canning found in the front of this section.

Vidalia Onion Jelly

Vidalia onions are sweet and flavorful. Try this jelly on your favorite meat or on a cold beef sandwich.

Ingredients:

⅔ c. Vidalia onion, grated
2 c. white wine vinegar
5½ c. sugar
3 c. water
2 oz. powdered pectin
1 tsp. butter
food coloring

Directions:

1. In a 2-quart saucepan, combine onions and vinegar.
2. Simmer mixture gently over medium heat for 15 minutes.
3. Remove pan from heat; pour vinegar mixture into a 1-quart glass jar; cover and leave at room temperature for 24 hours.
4. Pour contents through wire strainer into bowl.
5. Press onion with back of spoon to squeeze out liquid; discard onion pulp.
6. Measure liquid into bowl, adding vinegar if needed, to measure 1 cup.
7. Combine this vinegar solution with water in a 5 or 6-quart kettle; add pectin, stirring well.
8. Bring mixture to a boil over high heat, stirring constantly to avoid scorching.
9. Add sugar; stir well.
10. Bring mixture to full, rolling boil; add butter to reduce foaming.
11. Boil mixture hard for exactly 2 minutes, while continuing to stir.
12. Remove pan from heat, skim off foam and add food coloring if desired.
13. Pour jelly into prepared glasses.
14. Process following a basic guide for canning found in the front of this section.

Onion Delights Cookbook
A Collection of Onion Recipes
Cookbook Delights Series-Book 8

Main Dishes

Table of Contents

Page

Baked Onion Stuffed Pork Chops

My husband loves baked onion stuffed pork chops. Try this delicious recipe the next time you have company for dinner.

Ingredients:

- 4 rib pork chops, 2-inch, cut with a pocket
- 2 Tbs. butter
- ⅓ c. onion, finely chopped
- ½ c. celery, chopped
- 1½ c. soft bread cubes
- ¼ c. raisins
- 2 Tbs. parsley, chopped
- ½ tsp. dried marjoram leaves
- 1 tsp. salt
- ⅛ tsp. pepper
- 3 Tbs. apple juice
- 1 tsp. seasoned salt

Directions:

1. Preheat oven to 350 degrees F.
2. In skillet, melt butter; sauté onion and celery until tender; 8 minutes.
3. Add bread cubes and brown slightly; remove from heat.
4. Add raisins, parsley, marjoram, salt, pepper, and apple juice, tossing mixture lightly to combine.
5. Fill pockets of each chop with stuffing.
6. Stand chops on rib bones, side by side along rack in shallow roasting pan; sprinkle with seasoned salt.
7. Pour water to ½-inch depth in roasting pan; water should not touch rack.
8. Cover pan with foil.
9. Bake for 55 minutes.
10. Remove foil; bake uncovered an additional 20 to 25 minutes, or until chops are tender and brown.

Yields: 4 servings.

Beef and Sweet Onion Sandwiches

These man-size sandwiches are tasty and popular. They make a hearty entrée on a hot summer's day. Serve with assorted raw vegetables, and your favorite dip to complete the meal.

Ingredients:

12 oz. boneless beef sirloin, cut 1-inch thick, trimmed
½ tsp. black pepper, coarsely ground
2 tsp. canola oil
1 med. sweet onion, sliced
2 Tbs. Dijon mustard
1 c. red bell pepper, roasted or 4 oz. of a jar, drained
8 slices sourdough bread, cut 1-inch thick
1½ c. spinach or salad greens, torn
salt, to taste

Directions:

1. Sprinkle both sides of meat with pepper and salt; press in lightly.
2. In large skillet, over medium-high heat, cook meat 8 minutes, or until slightly pink in center, turning once.
3. Remove from skillet and keep warm.
4. Add onion to drippings in skillet, adding more oil if necessary.
5. Sauté 5 minutes, or until onion is crisp and tender.
6. Stir in mustard; remove from heat to cool.
7. Cut the roasted red peppers into ½-inch wide strips.
8. Toast bread, if desired, and shred spinach or salad greens.
9. Cut meat into thinly sliced bite-size strips.
10. When ready to serve, top 4 bread slices with spinach or salad greens, meat strips, roasted pepper strips, onion mixture, and top with remaining bread slices.

Beef Empanadas

Our family loves these as a main dish. Try them. They are worth the wait!

Ingredients:

2 Tbs. butter
½ c. onion, chopped
1 lb. ground beef or pork, extra lean
2 lg. ripe tomatoes, chopped
1 tsp. salt
3 oz. can green chilies, drained, chopped
1 bay leaf
2 Tbs. black olives, chopped

Ingredients for pastry:

1½ c. flour
¾ tsp. salt
½ c. butter
4 Tbs. cold water
1 egg yolk

Directions:

1. In large skillet, melt butter.
2. Sauté onion until tender.
3. Add ground beef or pork; sauté until well browned.
4. Add tomatoes, chilies, salt, and bay leaf.
5. Stir occasionally while simmering, 20 minutes, or until liquid has evaporated.
6. Remove from heat.
7. Discard bay leaf.
8. Stir in olives.
9. Set aside while making pastry.

Directions for pastry:

1. Preheat oven to 400 degrees F.

2. In medium bowl, combine flour, salt, butter, and water.
3. Blend until mixture clings together like bread dough.
4. Divide pastry into 12 pieces on lightly floured surface; roll each piece into a 6-inch round.
5. Place 3 tablespoons of filling on half of each round; fold over other half.
6. Press edges together with fingers to seal, flute edges.
7. Cut two small slits on top of each empanada.
8. Brush with egg yolk beaten with 1 tablespoon water.
9. Bake 20 to 25 minutes, or until golden brown.
10. Note: Packaged pastry mix can also be used and prepared as label directs; continue as in step 5.
11. For faster cooking, empanadas can also be deep fried in oil.

Greek Smelt and Onion Cake (Begoto)

This classic Greek recipe is wonderful for seafood fans and very easy to make. Try some tonight!

Ingredients:

very small smelt, cleaned, moistened
flour
onion, minced
olive oil
ouzo

Directions:

1. Dip several smelt at a time in a mixture of flour and minced onion.
2. Smelt should stick together and form cakes.
3. Fry in hot olive oil.
4. Remove and drain before serving.
5. Place cakes on serving plate and serve with ouzo, a Greek anise flavored liqueur.

Bordeaux Wine Stew with Maitake Mushrooms

I love Maitake mushrooms and onions. This combination is particularly delicious and makes a great family meal.

Ingredients for marinade:

2 c. water
2 c. dry red wine
1 cube beef bouillon
2 garlic cloves, crushed

Ingredients for stew:

1 lb. stew beef, cut into cubes
2 Tbs. butter
1 Tbs. canola oil
1 Tbs. flour
2 onions, evenly sliced
1 carrot, cut into bite-size pieces
4 potatoes, cut into bite-size pieces
1 cube beef bouillon
1 c. Maitake mushrooms
salt and pepper, to taste

Directions for marinade:

1. In medium bowl, mix water with the wine.
2. Add bouillon cube and garlic; blend well.
3. Place beef cubes in the marinade; let set for 3 hours to absorb mixture.

Directions for stew:

1. In wok, over high heat, place butter and oil; remove beef from marinade and drain.
2. Place beef in wok.

3. Sprinkle with flour while braising; when browned, place all in large stew pot.
4. Place onions and carrots in wok; stir-fry lightly and place with beef.
5. Add remaining marinade mixture and bouillon cube together.
6. Bring to a brief boil.
7. Pour into stew pot over beef and vegetables.
8. Boil all ingredients for 1½ hours.
9. In the wok with butter added, lightly stir-fry the Maitake mushrooms; add to stew after cooking is done.
10. Add salt and pepper to taste.
11. Ladle into individual serving bowls and serve with crusty bread for a real treat.

Country Steak and Onions

This is a classic country steak with onions that really adds to the delicious flavor.

Ingredients:

2 lb. round steak
2 Tbs. flour
2 Tbs. butter
1½ c. onions, sliced
1 c. water, boiling
salt and pepper, to taste

Directions:

1. Pound steak and rub with flour, salt, and pepper.
2. In large skillet, sauté onions in butter until browned.
3. Remove onions from pan; set aside.
4. Place beef in same skillet and brown on both sides.
5. Add onions back to the beef and pour in the water.
6. Cover; simmer slowly for 1 hour, or until tender.

Crab Cakes with Avocado and Onion Salsa

These crab cakes are absolutely delicious, and the salsa just adds more flavor. This salsa is very versatile and can be used with many dishes.

Ingredients for cakes:

3 eggs, beaten
4 Tbs. green onion, thinly sliced
1 Tbs. mayonnaise
2 Tbs. sweet chili sauce
1¼ c. fresh white bread crumbs
1¼ lb. Dungeness crabmeat, flaked
canola oil, for frying

Ingredients for salsa:

1 c. ripe Roma tomatoes, chopped
½ c. red onion, chopped
1 c. ripe avocado, finely diced
4 Tbs. fresh squeezed lime juice
2 Tbs. cilantro, roughly chopped
salt and pepper, to taste

Directions for cakes:

1. In medium bowl, combine eggs, onion, mayonnaise, and chili sauce; blend well.
2. Gently add bread crumbs and flaked crabmeat.
3. Cover with plastic wrap and refrigerate 30 minutes.
4. Using wet hands, form crab mixture into 12 small cakes.
5. Place on flat plate for ease in removing.
6. Heat 1¼ inches of oil in a heavy skillet until quite hot.
7. Gently slide cakes, one at a time, into hot oil.
8. Fry several at a time, 3 to 4 minutes per side, or until golden.
9. Drain on paper towels.
10. Serve these delicious crab cakes, hot, with the salsa.

Directions for salsa:

1. In medium bowl, combine tomato, onion, and avocado; blend well.
2. Add lime juice, cilantro, and salt and pepper to taste.
3. Let stand for 1 hour to blend flavors, if desired.
4. Serve with the hot crab cakes.

Italian Sausage, Onion, and Potato Casserole

This is a mildly spicy dish with meat, potatoes, and vegetables all in one. Serve with green salad and hot Italian biscuits for a hearty meal.

Ingredients:

1 lb. Italian sausage
2 lg. red potatoes, unpeeled, cut into 8 wedges
2 lg. sweet onions, cut into large cubes
1 lg. bell pepper, cut into large cubes
¼ tsp. onion salt
¼ tsp. garlic powder
1 tsp. basil
1 tsp. dill
1 tsp. oregano
½ tsp. pepper
butter

Directions:

1. Preheat oven to 400 degrees F.
2. Lightly butter a casserole dish with a cover.
3. Cut sausage into 2-inch pieces.
4. In large bowl, add sausage, potatoes, onions, and peppers.
5. Sprinkle with the seasonings and toss gently.
6. Spoon into prepared dish; cover.
7. Bake 1 hour, or until potatoes are tender.
8. Remove from oven; let sit for 10 minutes.

Green Onion Crab Cakes with Pineapple Salsa

This is a delicious, exotic crab cake. The pineapple salsa really complements it in a unique way.

Ingredients for crab cakes:

1 egg, beaten
2 green onions, chopped
2 Tbs. mayonnaise
1 Tbs. fresh parsley, chopped
½ tsp. Worcestershire sauce
1 dash hot pepper sauce
½ lb. fresh crabmeat
½ c. bread crumbs
black pepper, to taste

Ingredients for salsa:

2 c. fresh pineapple, diced or canned, drained well
½ c. green onions, chopped
¼ c. fresh cilantro, chopped
1 Tbs. fresh lemon juice
⅛ tsp. cayenne pepper
salt and pepper, to taste

Directions for crab cakes:

1. In medium bowl, combine eggs, onion, and mayonnaise.
2. Add parsley and hot pepper sauces; blend well.
3. Gently fold in crab and bread crumbs; season to taste with black pepper.
4. Cover and chill 15 minutes.
5. Form crab mixture into 8 patties of equal size.
6. Coat large nonstick skillet with canola cooking spray and set over medium-high heat.
7. Sauté crab cakes, turning once, until golden on both sides, 3 minutes per side.

8. Remove to serving dish and serve with pineapple salsa below.

Directions for salsa:

1. In medium bowl, combine pineapple, onion, and cilantro.
2. Add lemon juice and cayenne pepper; toss lightly.
3. Season with salt and pepper.

Onion Cheeseburger

My husband loves onion cheeseburgers. Having the onion minced into the meat ensures that great onion flavor in every bite.

Ingredients:

ground sirloin or ground beef
steak sauce
onions, minced
hot sauce
water
sliced cheese
hamburger buns
condiments, such as ketchup, mustard, and relish

Directions:

1. Put ground beef in large mixing bowl.
2. Pour steak sauce over beef, usually half of a 10-ounce bottle.
3. Sprinkle minced onions in the amount desired, over meat and knead together.
4. Once mixed well, make hamburger patties to desired size.
5. Put dash of hot sauce and water in skillet and sauté until meat is done.
6. Just before lifting out of pan, lay slices of cheese over each meat patty.
7. Place on warmed hamburger buns.
8. Add your favorite condiments.

Grilled Shish Kabobs with Onions

My daughter Marissa loves grilled shish kabobs with onions, and we try to make them often.

Ingredients for marinade:

⅓ c. soy sauce
¾ c. canola oil
⅛ c. hot sauce
1 Tbs. dry mustard
2 tsp. salt
1 tsp. parsley
1½ tsp. pepper, ground
1 garlic clove, crushed
¼ c. lemon juice

Ingredients for kabobs:

2½ lb. beef, cut into 2-inch squares
12 cherry tomatoes
12 sm. mushrooms
12 sm. onions
2 lg. green peppers, cut into 1-inch squares
3 slices bacon, each cut into 4 squares
2 sm. to med. zucchini, cut into slices

Directions for marinade:

1. In blender, combine soy sauce, oil, hot sauce, and dry mustard.
2. Blend lightly.
3. Add salt, parsley, ground pepper, garlic, and lemon juice.
4. Blend for 30 seconds.
5. Pour into jar with tight lid.
6. Refrigerate for several hours to blend flavors.

Directions for kabobs:

1. In large bowl, place beef squares in marinade for several hours or all day.
2. To prepare kabobs, arrange meat and vegetables in alternating order on skewers until skewer is full, ending with meat; brush with marinade.
3. Broil over hot coals 15 minutes, or until cooked.
4. Turn skewers and brush with marinade during the cooking process.
5. When roasted, place skewers with vegetables and meat intact onto large serving platters.

Pan-Fried Liver and Onions

This is a hearty, delicious meal that will leave your guests asking for more!

Ingredients:

3 Tbs. butter
2 med. sweet onions, thinly sliced
1 lb. beef, veal, or pork liver, ½ to ¾-inch thickness
3 Tbs. olive oil
flour
salt and pepper, to taste

Directions:

1. In large skillet, over medium-high heat, melt butter.
2. Cook onions in butter 4 to 6 minutes, stirring frequently, until light brown.
3. Remove onions from skillet; keep warm.
4. Dredge liver with flour.
5. Heat oil in same skillet over medium heat.
6. Cook liver in oil, 2 to 3 minutes on each side, or until brown and cooked through.
7. Sprinkle with salt and pepper, top with sautéed onions, and serve.

Sauerbraten

My husband lived in Germany and actually has some German heritage, so I try to share these traditions with our blended family. This is a delicious way to prepare your beef roast for a Sunday supper.

Ingredients:

4 lb. boneless chuck or rump roast
2 c. wine vinegar
2 c. water
1 garlic clove
¾ c. onion, sliced
1 bay leaf
10 peppercorns
¼ c. sugar
3 whole cloves
2 Tbs. bacon drippings
1½ c. sour cream
salt and pepper, to taste
flour

Directions:

1. In large bowl, season meat with salt and pepper.
2. In medium saucepan, bring vinegar and water to a boil.
3. Add garlic, onion, bay leaf, peppercorns, sugar, and cloves.
4. Pour marinade over beef.
5. Cover and refrigerate twelve hours or overnight.
6. Remove meat and dry thoroughly with paper towels; reserve marinade.
7. Dredge meat with flour.
8. In Dutch oven, heat bacon drippings.
9. Add meat; brown on all sides.
10. Add 2 cups of the marinade and cover tightly.
11. Simmer gently for 2½ to 3 hours, or until meat is tender.
12. Remove meat to warm platter.

13. Slice, cover and keep hot.
14. Thicken drippings with a little flour mixed with water to make gravy.
15. Stir in sour cream.
16. Serve gravy over sliced meat.

Stir-fry Mushrooms and Beef with Oyster Sauce

This stir-fry has a very complex, interesting flavor. Maitake mushrooms add great flavor to this delicious dish!

Ingredients:

8 oz. Maitake mushrooms
8 oz. beef, sliced into strips
1 c. soy sauce
1 c. white wine
1 Tbs. canola oil
1 red pepper, diced
2 shoots scallions, cut to desired size
1 sm. eggplant, cut to desired size
2 leaves Chinese cabbage, sliced into 1-inch strips
3 Tbs. oyster juice

Directions:

1. Break mushrooms into bite-size portions.
2. In small bowl, marinate beef in soy sauce and wine for 5 to 6 minutes.
3. Heat oil in wok on high heat.
4. Add beef strips.
5. Stir-fry for 1 minute.
6. Add red pepper, scallions, and eggplant.
7. Stir-fry for 1 minute.
8. Add mushrooms, Chinese cabbage, and oyster juice.
9. Stir-fry 3 minutes, until just tender.
10. Serve with a plate of rice or noodles.
11. Add a green salad for a lovely meal.

Poached Chicken with Onion, Rice, and Ginger Relish

The herbs and seasonings add refreshing flavors to this savory chicken and rice dish.

Ingredients for ginger relish:

2 Tbs. ginger, cut into matchsticks
8 green onions, finely sliced
1 Tbs. cilantro, chopped
¼ c. canola oil
salt and pepper, to taste

Ingredients for chicken and rice:

3⅓ lb. chicken, excess fat removed
1 bunch cilantro, chopped (¼ of sprigs reserved)
3 green onions, chopped
1 tsp. black peppercorns
2 Tbs. salt
2¼ c. long-grain rice
1 Tbs. canola oil
1 Tbs. sesame oil
1 Tbs. garlic, crushed
1 Tbs. ginger, grated
1 med. onion, finely sliced
8 c. water
fresh ginger relish (see below)

Directions for ginger relish:

1. In medium bowl, place ginger and green onions.
2. Lightly bruise by hitting with wooden spoon.
3. Add a tablespoon of chopped cilantro.
4. Heat oil in pan just until smoking.
5. Pour over ginger mixture, while tossing, into a heatproof bowl.

6. Season to taste.
7. Set aside to blend while preparing chicken dish.

Directions for chicken and rice:

1. In a 4-quart pot, place chicken.
2. Add remaining cilantro, green onions, peppercorns, salt, and 8 cups of water; bring to boil.
3. Reduce heat to low-simmer.
4. Cover pot and continue to simmer 25 minutes.
5. Remove from heat.
6. Leave chicken in pot for 40 minutes more, without lifting lid.
7. Lift chicken out onto a platter.
8. Wash rice until water until it runs clear.
9. Heat oils in saucepan over low heat.
10. Add garlic, ginger, and onion.
11. Stir-fry for 3 minutes.
12. Add rice and the chicken liquid to pot; bring to a boil and cook 15 minutes.
13. Cover; reduce heat to low.
14. Cut chicken into serving-size pieces and place back into pot; simmer 15 minutes.
15. Remove from heat.
16. Let stand 10 minutes without lifting lid to absorb liquid.
17. Season with salt and pepper before serving.
18. Gently lift the chicken out of pot onto platter.
19. Decorate with sprigs of cilantro.
20. Place onion, rice, and fresh ginger relish into separate serving dishes.
21. Serve with a bowl of sliced cucumber on the side.

Did You Know? . . . .

Did you know that it was once believed that an onion rubbed on your head was said to cure baldness? The onion juice was supposed to cause the hair to grow "thick as thistles." Note: You may have to sleep alone, but at least you will have hair!

Onion and Bacon Tart

This is a great way to use up any onions you have around the house, while making a delicious meal!

Ingredients for dough:

2 c. flour
1 tsp. salt
1 tsp. canola oil
¾ c. water (approximate)

Ingredients for filling:

12 slices bacon, cut into ½-inch pieces
4 med. onions, thinly sliced
4 c. cottage cheese, puréed until almost smooth
5 Tbs. whipping cream
1 Tbs. canola oil
½ tsp. salt
¼ tsp. nutmeg
¼ tsp. pepper

Directions for dough:

1. In medium bowl, combine flour, salt, oil, and enough water to make a soft dough.
2. Blend together until dough clings.
3. Turn onto a lightly floured surface.
4. Knead until smooth and elastic, 3 minutes.
5. Wrap dough in plastic.
6. Chill in refrigerator for several hours or overnight.
7. Let warm to room temperature before dividing and rolling.

Directions for filling:

1. Preheat oven to 500 degrees F.

2. In skillet, over medium heat, brown bacon.
3. Remove from pan and drain on paper towels.
4. Cook onions in bacon fat until light brown and soft, 10 minutes.
5. In small bowl, blend cottage cheese, whipping cream, oil, salt, and spices well; set aside.
6. Divide dough into quarters.
7. Roll each into a 12-inch circle.
8. Place on pizza pan or baking sheets.
9. Cover each with a quarter of the cream mixture.
10. Sprinkle top with a quarter of the bacon and onions.
11. Bake on lower rack in oven for 12 minutes, or until bubbly and slightly brown.

Swedish Meatballs

This is a family favorite. Serve with boiled new potatoes and a vegetable or serve on top of your favorite spaghetti.

Ingredients:

½ c. half and half cream
1 lb. ground beef
¼ c. cracker crumbs
½ tsp. salt
⅛ tsp. pepper
1 sm. onion
1 egg
¼ tsp. celery seeds
⅛ tsp. nutmeg

Directions:

1. Preheat oven to 350 degrees F.
2. In large bowl, combine all ingredients.
3. Mix well.
4. Roll into balls 1-inch in diameter.
5. Bake 25 to 30 minutes.

Swiss Steak with Onions

My mom used to make Swiss steak, and it was one of my favorite meals. My family really enjoys it served with mashed potatoes or rigatoni noodles.

Ingredients:

3 lb. round steak, cut ¾-inch thick
⅔ c. flour
1 Tbs. salt
½ tsp. pepper
⅛ c. olive oil
⅛ c. butter
½ c. onions, sliced in rings
1 qt. water
1 c. half and half cream

Directions:

1. Preheat oven to 325 degrees F.
2. Pound flour, salt, and pepper into steak.
3. Reserve remaining flour mixture.
4. Cut steak into 10 serving-size pieces.
5. Melt butter with oil in a large heavy skillet.
6. Brown onions lightly.
7. Transfer to large roasting pan.
8. Brown meat well on both sides.
9. Transfer to roasting pan.
10. Add remaining flour mixture to skillet; stir to brown.
11. Slowly add water and cream.
12. Simmer, stirring about 5 minutes.
13. Pour over steak.
14. Cover pan.
15. Bake for 2 to 2½ hours, or until meat is fork tender.

Pies

Table of Contents

A Basic Recipe for Pie Crust

This is a very good recipe for a delicious, flaky crust.

Ingredients for single crust:

1½ c. sifted all-purpose flour
½ tsp. salt
½ c. shortening
4-5 Tbs. ice water

Ingredients for double crust:

2 c. sifted all-purpose flour
1 tsp. salt
⅔ c. shortening
5-7 Tbs. ice water

Directions for single crust:

1. In large bowl stir together flour and salt.
2. Cut in shortening with pastry blender or mix with fingertips until pieces are size of coarse crumbs.
3. Sprinkle 2 tablespoons ice water over flour mixture, tossing with fork.
4. Add just enough remaining water 1 tablespoon at a time to moisten dough, tossing so dough holds together.
5. Roll pastry into 11-inch circle, and wrap in plastic wrap; refrigerate for 1 hour.
6. Preheat oven to 425 degrees F.
7. Remove plastic wrap from pastry, and fit pastry into a 9-inch pie plate.
8. Fold edge under and then crimp between thumb and forefinger to make fluted crust.
9. For filled pie with an instant or cooked filling (cream-filled, custard-filled, etc.), prick crust all over with fork then bake 15 to 20 minutes until done.
10. If preparing pie with uncooked filling (such as pumpkin), do not prick crust; pour filling into unbaked pastry shell, and then bake as directed.

Directions for double crust:

1. Turn desired filling into pastry-lined pie plate; trim overhanging edge of pastry ½ inch from rim of plate.
2. Cut slits with knife in top crust for steam vents.
3. Place over filling; trim overhanging edge of pastry 1 inch from rim of plate.
4. Fold and roll top edge under lower edge, pressing on rim to seal; flute.
5. Cover fluted edge with 2- to 3-inch-wide strip of aluminum foil to prevent excessive browning.
6. Remove foil during last 15 minutes of baking.

Yields: 1 pie crust (9-inch single or double).

A Basic Cookie or Graham Cracker Crust

This is a great crust for use with cream pies or for an unbaked pie. Use your favorite flavor of cookie to complement your filling, or use graham crackers.

Ingredients:

2 c. cookie or graham cracker crumbs, finely crushed
⅓ c. sugar
½ c. butter, melted

Directions:

1. Combine crumbs, sugar, and butter.
2. Press mixture firmly against bottom and up sides of 9-inch pie plate.
3. Baking is not necessary, but if preferred crust may be baked at 400 degrees F. for 10 minutes.

Yields: 1 pie crust (9-inch).

Calzones with Onions

Calzones are a family favorite and worth the extra time to prepare.

Ingredients for crust:

- 2 tsp. sugar
- 2 tsp. active dry yeast
- 1 c. water, warm
- ¾ tsp. salt
- 2½ c. flour
- 2 Tbs. olive oil

Ingredients for filling:

- 1 can tomato sauce (8 oz.)
- 1 tsp. basil leaves
- 1 tsp. oregano leaves
- 2 Italian pork sausages
- 4 Tbs. olive oil, divided
- 1 lg. onion, chopped
- 2¼ c. mozzarella cheese, freshly shredded
- 1½ c. Romano or Parmesan cheese, freshly shredded
- water

Directions for crust:

1. In small cup, mix yeast and sugar with ½ cup warm water.
2. Let sit for 5 minutes to allow yeast to soften and mixture to become frothy or bubbly.
3. Add salt, remaining water and half the flour; beat this mixture into a batter.
4. Slowly add rest of the flour into the batter by kneading in with your hands until all the flour has been incorporated, and has become a ball of dough.
5. Turn out onto a floured surface.

6. Knead for 3 to 5 minutes, or until dough becomes smooth and elastic.
7. Place olive oil in a large bowl.
8. Roll dough in the oil until coated.
9. Cover and allow rising until double in bulk.
10. Make calzone filling while dough is rising.

Directions for filling:

1. In small saucepan, heat tomato sauce with basil and oregano; set aside.
2. Simmer sausages in enough water to cover for 20 minutes; drain, cool, remove casings, and slice thinly.
3. Divide dough into portions for calzones desired and compress each into flat cake.
4. Roll each out to a 10 or 11-inch circle.
5. Let stand for 10 minutes, and brush lightly using half of the oil.
6. Evenly divide filling ingredients to equal dough portions.
7. Preheat oven to 500 degrees F.
8. Lightly grease a baking sheet.
9. Spread tomato sauce over half the dough circle to within ½ inch of edge.
10. Top sauce with sausage and onion.
11. Sprinkle with mozzarella and Romano cheese.
12. Fold plain half over filling to within ¼ inch of opposite edge.
13. Roll bottom edge up over top edge; pinch or crimp together to seal.
14. Place on prepared baking sheet.
15. Brush with oil and lightly prick calzone with fork to let steam escape.
16. Depending on how many calzones you are making from the recipe, place half of them at a time on a baking sheet or use two sheets.
17. Bake 6 to 10 minutes, or until golden brown.

Caraway Onion Pie

Caraway seeds add great flavor to this onion pie. If you like, try adding some grated cheese.

Ingredients:

6 med. onions, sliced, select your favorite
3 Tbs. butter
4 eggs
½ c. flour
1 tsp. salt
1 tsp. caraway seeds
2 c. milk
½ c. Cheddar cheese, grated
1 single pastry crust (recipe in front of this section)
pepper, to taste

Directions:

1. Preheat oven to 350 degrees F.
2. In medium skillet, melt butter.
3. Sauté onions until cooked but not brown.
4. In small bowl, combine eggs, flour, salt, and caraway seeds.
5. Add milk and stir in cooked onions.
6. Pour into an unbaked pie shell.
7. Sprinkle with grated cheese.
8. Bake for 1 hour, or until knife inserted in center comes out clean.
9. Remove from oven; cool slightly.
10. Slice to serve.

Did You Know? . . . .

Did you know that it is said you can use two ounces of an equal measure of raw garlic and onion juice, and it may restore hearing?

Cheese and Onion Pie

This savory pie makes a great first course and is good served warm or at room temperature.

Ingredients:

3 lb. onions, sliced
3 Tbs. butter
3 eggs
1 pt. heavy cream
1 pinch nutmeg
½ c. Cheddar cheese, grated
1 double crust pastry (recipe in front of this section)
salt and pepper, to taste

Directions:

1. Preheat oven to 350 degrees F.
2. In skillet, melt butter and sauté onions.
3. Allow to cool for a few minutes.
4. In small bowl, beat together eggs and cream.
5. Add nutmeg, cheese, and salt and pepper to taste.
6. Line deep pie plate with one of the pie crusts.
7. Add onion to creamed mixture.
8. Pour into pie shell and top with second crust.
9. Pinch edges to seal; cut slits in top crust for steam vents.
10. Bake 1 hour, or until crust is golden brown, and a knife inserted in center comes out clean.
11. Remove from oven, cool slightly and slice to serve.

Yields: 6 servings.

Did You Know?....

Did you know that the official state vegetable of Texas is the Texas Sweet Onion?

Creamy Onion Pie

This recipe makes a delicious, savory onion pie.

Ingredients:

- 6 Tbs. butter
- 3 med. sweet onions, sliced
- ½ c. flour
- 2 c. sweetened whipping cream
- 6 Tbs. sour cream
- 1¼ c. Cheddar cheese, shredded
- 1 deep-dish pastry crust (recipe in front of this section)
- salt and pepper, to taste

Directions:

1. Preheat oven to 350 degrees F.
2. In skillet, over medium heat, melt butter and sauté onions until tender, but not brown; 8 to 10 minutes.
3. Sprinkle flour over onions stirring until evenly coated.
4. Stirring constantly, slowly pour in cream.
5. Remove from heat.
6. Add sour cream, season to taste with salt and pepper.
7. Pour into unbaked pie shell.
8. Sprinkle cheese evenly over top.
9. Bake 45 minutes, until crust is golden with cheese melted and slightly brown.
10. Remove from oven.
11. Cool completely until mixture is firm enough to slice.
12. If desired, preheat each portion just before serving.

Yields: 8 servings.

Delicious Onion and Bacon Pie

Onion, chives, and bacon combine to make a tasty onion pie. Serve warm and enjoy!

Ingredients:

12 slices bacon
2 c. onions, thinly sliced
3 Tbs. bacon drippings
1 c. sour cream
4 eggs, slightly beaten
1½ tsp. chives, chopped
1 single pastry crust (recipe in front of this section)
½ tsp. caraway seeds
salt and pepper, to taste

Directions:

1. Preheat oven to 325 degrees F.
2. In skillet, fry bacon slices until crisp.
3. Drain on paper towels.
4. Crumble bacon and reserve drippings.
5. Sauté onions in drippings until slightly translucent.
6. In small bowl, beat sour cream and eggs.
7. Add chives, onions, and salt and pepper to taste.
8. Pour into pie shell.
9. Sprinkle caraway seeds and half of the crumbled bacon to top.
10. Bake for 35 minutes, or until knife inserted in center comes out clean.
11. Remove from oven; top with remainder of crumbled bacon; let stand 10 minutes before cutting to serve.

Did You Know?....

Did you know that if you eat onions, you can get rid of onion breath by eating parsley?

Deep-Dish Onion Pizza Pie

This is a truly delicious pizza pie. Try experimenting by adding your favorite topping.

Ingredients for crust:

2 Tbs. white cornmeal
1 pkg. active dry yeast
1 tsp. sugar
½ c. water, warm
3 c. flour
1½ tsp. salt
3 Tbs. olive oil

Ingredients for filling:

1 lb. Italian sausage
2 med. onions, sliced
1 lg. green pepper or half red and green, sliced
6 oz. mushrooms, sliced
1 c. black olives, chopped
3 Tbs. flour
1½ tsp. fennel, finely ground
1½ tsp. dried oregano
1 tsp. dried red pepper flakes
1¼ tsp. salt
1 lb. mozzarella cheese, shredded
½ lb. white Cheddar cheese, grated
2 Tbs. olive oil

Ingredients for sauce:

4 med. whole tomatoes, peeled, puréed
1 c. tomato sauce
¼ c. tomato paste
⅛ tsp. salt
⅛ tsp. black pepper, freshly ground
1 tsp. sugar
1 tsp. dried oregano
1 tsp. dried basil

Directions for crust:

1. Grease a 14-inch deep-dish pie pan; sprinkle with cornmeal.
2. In small bowl, mix yeast, sugar, and warm water.
3. Let stand 10 minutes until bubbly.
4. Add flour, salt, and oil; knead until smooth.
5. If dough is too sticky, add more flour, 1 tablespoon at a time, until consistency is correct.
6. Place dough into oiled bowl; cover with plastic wrap.
7. Refrigerate 1 to 10 hours.

Directions for filling:

1. Remove all meat from casings and brown, breaking into pieces; drain.
2. Using same pan, sauté onion, peppers, and mushrooms; add sausage back to mixture.
3. To this mixture, add olives, flour, spices, and salt; blend well.
4. Reserve cheese and oil until assembly.

Directions for sauce:

1. In medium bowl, combine tomatoes, sauce, and paste; mix well.
2. Add salt, pepper, sugar, and spices; blend well. Set aside.

Directions for assembly:

1. Preheat oven to 425 degrees F.
2. Roll out dough on floured surface until elastic.
3. Place in greased pan with cornmeal, leaving a high rim all around.
4. Toss cheeses together and then place half of the cheese directly on dough, followed by filling, with sauce on top; sprinkle remaining cheeses over top.
5. Bake for 45 to 50 minutes, or until done.

German Onion Pie (Zweibel kuchen)

This is a traditional German recipe that will have your guests asking for more!

Ingredients:

4 thick slices bacon, diced
2 c. yellow onions, peeled, chopped
2 eggs, beaten
1 c. sour cream
½ tsp. salt
¼ tsp. black pepper, freshly ground
1 Tbs. flour
1 single pastry crust (recipe in front of this section)

Directions:

1. Preheat oven to 400 degrees F.
2. In skillet, sauté bacon; drain off and discard all but 1 tablespoon of grease from pan.
3. Add onions and sauté until clear; do not brown; set aside to cool.
4. In medium bowl, beat eggs and sour cream together; add salt and pepper.
5. Sprinkle flour over top and beat well.
6. Spread onions and bacon over bottom of pie shell.
7. Pour sour cream mixture over top.
8. Bake for 15 minutes.
9. Reduce heat to 350 degrees F.
10. Bake another 15 minutes, or until pie is nicely browned.
11. Remove from oven.
12. Slice into serving size pieces.
13. Serve hot.

Yields: 6 to 8 servings.

Minced Beef and Onion Pie

A savory combination of beef and onions makes a hearty and tasty pie.

Ingredients:

2 Tbs. canola oil
1 lg. onion, diced
1 lb. minced beef
1 pt. water
3 beef bouillon cubes
3 Tbs. hot sauce
1 double pastry crust (recipe in front of this section)
1 Tbs. milk, for brushing pastry

Directions:

1. In large skillet, heat oil.
2. Gently fry onions until translucent.
3. Add minced beef to pan and break up with fork.
4. Add water, making sure beef is completely covered; bring to boil.
5. Crumble in bouillon cubes; add hot sauce.
6. Cover pan and reduce heat, simmering gently for 20 minutes.
7. When beef and onions are cooked, allow to cool for 15 minutes.
8. Preheat oven to 375 degrees F.
9. Roll out pastry on floured surface and use half to line a 9-inch round shallow baking pan.
10. Make pastry lid using remaining pastry.
11. Put beef and onion mixture in prepared pan; cover with pastry lid.
12. Flute around edges to seal; cut several small slits in center of pastry lid for steam vents; brush pastry with milk.
13. Bake for 30 minutes.
14. Remove from oven and let cool slightly before slicing to serve.
15. Add a salad to make a light and delicious meal.

Savory Onion Pie

This delicious onion pie served along side of a main dish is great for lunch or dinner.

Ingredients for crust:

½ tsp. salt
2 c. flour
4 tsp. baking powder
1 c. shortening
¾ c. milk

Ingredients for filling:

2 Tbs. butter
2 c. onions, sliced vertically
1 egg
¾ c. sour cream
salt and pepper, to taste

Directions for crust:

1. In large bowl, stir together flour, baking powder, and salt.
2. Cut shortening into mixture until it has texture of coarse crumbs.
3. Add milk to form dough.
4. Press dough into a 10 x 10-inch baking dish.

Directions for filling:

1. Preheat oven to 450 degrees F.
2. In skillet, sauté onion in butter until golden, but not brown.
3. Spread onion mixture over dough.
4. In small bowl, beat together egg and sour cream.
5. Season with salt and pepper to taste.
6. Pour into prepared crust.
7. Bake 20 minutes, or until knife inserted in center comes out clean.

8. Remove from oven, cool slightly and cut into squares to serve.

Sweet Onion Pie

This sweet onion pie differs from others with the addition of feta cheese.

Ingredients:

2 Tbs. canola oil
3 lg. sweet onions, sliced
2 Tbs. white cooking wine
2 eggs, beaten
3 Tbs. fresh parsley, chopped, divided
1 Tbs. fresh dill, chopped, or 1 tsp. dried
½ tsp. dried tarragon
4 oz. feta cheese, crumbled
salt and pepper, to taste
fine dry bread crumbs

Directions:

1. Preheat oven to 350 degrees F.
2. Lightly spray a 9-inch springform or tart pan with cooking spray.
3. Line bottom generously with bread crumbs.
4. Heat oil in skillet.
5. Sauté onions, 5 minutes.
6. Add wine; continue to sauté until golden; about 15 minutes.
7. Combine eggs with 2 tablespoons of parsley, dill, tarragon, cheese, and salt and pepper; stir in sautéed onions.
8. Pour onion mixture over top and sprinkle with remaining parsley and light layer of crumbs.
9. Bake 40 to 45 minutes, or until top is golden.
10. Remove from oven.
11. Let stand 5 minutes before slicing to serve.

Three-Onion Pot Pie

Pot pies are always great to have in the freezer. Make ahead and pull them out on a busy night.

Ingredients for pie:

½ c. butter
2 c. white onions, diced
2 c. red onions, diced
2 c. yellow onions, diced
2 c. carrots, peeled, thick sliced
3 c. mushrooms, quartered
2 c. celery, thick sliced
1½ c. red bell peppers, diced
4 c. boneless, skinless chicken meat, diced
¾ c. flour
4½ c. prepared pie crust dough (36 oz.)

Ingredients for sauce:

½ c. dark beer
1½ c. cream
2 c. chicken broth
1 Tbs. chicken base
2 Tbs. fresh thyme, minced
¼ c. parsley, minced
¾ c. fresh basil, chopped
2 tsp. garlic, minced
1 c. green onions, finely sliced
½ tsp. black pepper
1½ tsp. salt

Directions for pie and sauce:

1. Preheat oven to 375 degrees F.
2. Lightly grease 12 individual baking dishes.

3. In a large, heavy saucepan, combine butter, all onions, carrots, mushrooms, celery, and red peppers.
4. Place over medium-high heat.
5. Add chicken and cook 10 minutes, stirring often.
6. Add flour and stir well to combine with vegetables.
7. For sauce: In large bowl, combine beer, cream, chicken broth and base, thyme, parsley, and basil; mix well to blend.
8. Add garlic, onions, and salt and pepper to taste.
9. Bring to simmer, stirring frequently.
10. Cook 10 minutes longer.
11. Place 1¼ cups of the filling in each of the prepared baking dishes.
12. Set aside to cool slightly.
13. Divide dough into 12 equal pieces.
14. Roll each piece into a disc to slightly overlap the baking dishes.
15. Place rolled dough over cooled filling.
16. Crimp edges slightly over rims to seal.
17. Cut three small slits into the top of each for steam vents.
18. Bake for 45 minutes, until crust is browned.
19. Remove from oven and serve immediately.
20. Note: If serving later, cool, then reheat in a 350 degrees F. oven for 15 to 20 minutes until heated through.
21. Make sure to cover loosely with foil to prevent burning the crust.

Yields: 12 pies.

Did You Know? . . . .

Did you know that 1 teaspoon of onion powder is equivalent to 1 tablespoon of dried onions? Either one is equivalent to about ⅓ cup of chopped onions.

Walla Walla Sweet Onion Pizza Pie

Our family loves pizza, and this one is excellent. Be sure to make enough for second servings. It goes fast!

Ingredients for dough:

1 c. water, very warm, not hot
1 pkg. active dry yeast
1 tsp. sugar
1 Tbs. plus 1½ tsp. extra virgin olive oil
3 c. flour
1 tsp. salt

Ingredients for topping:

5 c. Walla Walla sweet onions, sliced
1 garlic clove, minced
¼ c. olive oil
½ tsp. oregano
1 c. pizza sauce, (8 oz.)
½ lb. Italian sausage, boiled, sliced
1 c. pitted black olives
2 Tbs. Parmesan cheese, grated
salt and pepper, to taste

Directions for dough:

1. In large bowl, combine water, yeast, sugar, and 1 tablespoon oil; stir to combine.
2. Let sit until mixture is foamy, about 5 minutes.
3. Add 1½ cups of the flour and 1 teaspoon salt.
4. Mix by hand until incorporated and mixture is smooth.
5. Continue adding flour, ¼ cup at a time, working dough after each addition, until all flour is incorporated but dough is still slightly sticky.
6. Turn dough out onto lightly floured surface.

7. Knead until smooth but still slightly tacky, 3 to 5 minutes.
8. Oil large mixing bowl with remaining 1½ teaspoons olive oil.
9. Place dough in bowl and turn to oil all sides of dough.
10. Cover bowl with plastic wrap.
11. Set in a warm place for 1 to 1½ hours, until nearly doubled in size.
12. Grease a 14-inch pizza pan.
13. After dough rises, line pan with dough, making a rim.

Directions for topping and assembly:

1. Preheat oven to 425 degrees F.
2. In large skillet, over low heat, add oil.
3. Sauté onion and garlic, until onion is translucent and tender.
4. Season with salt, pepper, and oregano.
5. Cool.
6. Layer pizza sauce and onion filling over crust.
7. Top with sausage, olives, and cheese.
8. Bake on bottom rack 20 to 30 minutes, or until crust is golden and cheese is bubbly.

Did You Know? . . . .

Did you know that the warmer the climate, the sweeter the onion?

Did you know that Grants Pass, Oregon, has a special ordinance making it perfectly legal for any citizen to throw onions at "obnoxious salesmen" when they won't stop knocking on the door or ringing the bell?

Did you know that in Tamarack, Idaho, no one can buy onions after dark with a special permit from the sheriff?

Onion Brie Pie

This makes a rich pie that is great to serve at your next dinner party.

Ingredients:

- 3 lb. onions, sliced
- 3 Tbs. butter
- 3 eggs
- 1 pt. heavy cream
- 1 pinch nutmeg
- ½ c. Brie, cut into sm. cubes
- 1 double pastry crust, (recipe in front of this section)
  salt and pepper, to taste

Directions:

1. Preheat oven to 350 degrees F.
2. In skillet, sauté onions in butter until translucent.
3. Allow to cool for a few minutes.
4. In small bowl, beat together eggs and cream; blend well.
5. Add nutmeg, onions, and cheese.
6. Line a deep pie plate with pastry.
7. Pour mixture into pie shell.
8. Place the top crust and flute the edges to seal.
9. Cut slits for steam vents.
10. Bake 1 hour, or until knife inserted in center comes out clean and crust is golden brown.
11. Remove from oven.
12. Cool slightly before slicing to serve.

Did You Know? . . . .

Did you know that if your rub your fingers with salt and vinegar, it will remove onion odors from your hands?

Onion Delights Cookbook
A Collection of Onion Recipes
Cookbook Delights Series-Book 8

Preserving

Table of Contents

A Basic Guide for Canning, Dehydrating, and Freezing

1. Place empty jars in hot, soapy water. Wash well inside and out with brush or soft cloth.
2. Run your finger around rim of each jar, discarding any that are chipped or cracked.
3. Rinse in clean, clear, very hot water, being careful to use tongs to avoid burning skin or fingers.
4. Place upside down on towel or fabric to drain well.
5. Place lids in boiling water bath for 2 minutes to sterilize and keep hot until ready to place on jar rims.
6. Immediately prior to filling jars with hot food, immerse in hot bath for 1 minute to heat jars. Heating jars avoids breakage.
7. If filling with room-temperature food, you need not immerse immediately prior to filling.
8. Fill jars with food to within ½ inch of neck of jars.
9. When ladling liquid over food, fill jars to 1 inch from top rim in each jar. This leaves air allowance for sealing purposes.
10. Wipe rims of jars with damp, clean cloth to remove any particles of food and again check for chips or cracks.
11. Using tongs, place lids from hot bath directly onto jars.
12. Place rings over lids, and using cloth, gloves, or holders, tighten down firmly while hanging onto jars.
13. Do not tighten down too hard as air may become trapped in jars and prevent them from sealing.
14. For fruits, tomatoes, and pickled vegetables, place each jar into water bath canning kettle so water covers jars by at least 1 inch.
15. For vegetables, process them in a pressure canner according to manufacturer's directions.
16. Follow time recommended for food being canned.
17. Do not mix jars of food in same canning kettle as times may vary for each kind of food.

18. At end of time recommended for canning, gently lift each jar out of bath with tongs, and place on protected surface.
19. Turn lids gently to be sure they are firmly tight.
20. Place filled, ringed jars on cloth to cool gradually.
21. Do not disturb rings, lids, or jars until sealed.
22. Lids will show slight indentation when sealed.
23. When cool, wipe jars with damp cloth then label and date each jar.
24. Leave overnight until thoroughly cooled.
25. Jars may then be stored upright on shelves.

Dehydrating

1. Always begin with fresh, good quality food that is clean and inspected for damage.
2. Pretreatment is not necessary, but food that is blanched will keep its color and flavor better. Use the same blanching times as you would for freezing. Fruit, especially, responds to pretreatment.
3. Doing some research on pretreatments may help you decide what procedure you would like to use.
4. You can marinate, salt, sweeten, or spice foods before you dehydrate them.
5. Jerky is meat that has been marinated and/or flavored by rubbing spices into it; avoid oil or grease of any kind as it will turn rancid as the food dries.
6. Vegetables and fruit can be treated the same way.
7. Slice or dice food thin and uniform so that it will dehydrate evenly. Uneven thicknesses may cause food to spoil because it did not dry as thoroughly as other parts.
8. Space food on dehydrator tray so that air can move around each piece.
9. Try not to let any piece touch another.
10. Fill your trays with all the same type of food as different foods take different amounts of time to dry.

11. You can, of course, dry different types of food at the same time, but you will have to remember to watch and remove the food that dehydrates more quickly. You can mix different foods in the same dehydrator batch, but do not mix strong vegetables like onions and garlic as other foods will absorb their taste while they are dehydrating.
12. The smaller the pieces, the faster a food will dehydrate. Thin leaves of spinach, celery, etc., will dry fastest. Remove them from the stalks before drying them or they will be overdone, losing flavor and quality. In very warm areas, they might even scorch. If they do, they will taste just like burned food when you rehydrate them.
13. Dense food like carrots will feel very hard when they are ready. Others will be crispy. Usually, a food that is high in fructose (sugar) will be leathery when it is finished dehydrating.
14. Remember that food smells when it is in the process of drying, so outdoors or in the garage is an excellent place to dry a big batch of those onions!
15. Always test each batch to make sure it is "done."
16. You can pasteurize finished food by putting it in a slow oven (150 degrees F.) for a few minutes.
17. Let the food cool before storing.
18. Store in airtight containers to guard against moisture. Jars saved from other food work well as long as they have lids that will keep moisture out.
19. Zip-closure food storage bags work well.
20. Jars of dehydrated carrots, celery, beets, etc., may look cheerful on your countertop, but the colors and flavors will fade. Dehydrated food keeps its color and flavor best if stored in a dark, cool place.
21. Dehydrating food takes time, so do not rush it. When you are all done, you will have a dried food stash to be proud of!

Freezing

1. Wash all containers and lids in hot, soapy water using soft cloth.
2. Rinse well in clear, clean, hot water.
3. Cool and drain well.
4. Place food into container to within 1 inch of rim. This allows for expansion of food during freezing.
5. Wipe rim of container with clean damp cloth, checking for chips or breaks.
6. Be certain cover fits the container snugly to avoid leaks. Burp air from container.
7. If food is hot when placing in container, cool prior to placing in freezer.
8. Label and date each container.
9. Store upright in freezer until frozen solid.

Onion Butter

Sesame oil adds wonderful flavor to this onion butter. Try it on your favorite bread or crackers. It is also delicious on vegetables, meats, or almost any foods desired.

Ingredients:

10 c. onions, chopped
1 pinch of sea salt
dark sesame oil
water

Directions:

1. In heavy pot, heat small amount of dark sesame oil.
2. Over medium-low heat, sauté onions for several minutes until translucent.
3. Stir often to sauté evenly.
4. Add a pinch of salt and just enough water to cover top of onions.
5. Cover pot and bring to boil.
6. Reduce heat to low.
7. Simmer several hours until onions become dark brown and very sweet. There should not be any liquid left; check often to prevent drying.
8. If necessary, add very small amounts of water occasionally during the cooking process to keep onions from burning.
9. Cool.
10. Process following a basic guide for canning, dehydrating, and freezing foods found at the beginning of this section.
11. After opening, butter can be refrigerated for up to 1 week.

Bread and Butter Pickles

My aunt used to can many bread and butter pickles, and they are great to have on your pantry shelf.

Ingredients:

8 lb. cucumbers, thinly sliced
1 lb. onions, sliced thin
2 gal. water
2 c. pickling lime
9 c. sugar
2 Tbs. salt
2 Tbs. celery seed
2 Tbs. pickling spice
8 c. vinegar
6 c. water

Directions:

1. In a large pot, soak cucumbers and onions in a mixture of 2 gallons water and 2 cups pickling lime for 24 hours.
2. Stir a few times throughout soaking time.
3. Rinse well.
4. Let stand in ice water for 3 hours.
5. Drain well.
6. In large pot, mix together sugar, salt, celery seed, pickling spice, vinegar, and water to make syrup.
7. Add cucumber and onion slices.
8. Cook 1½ hours.
9. Process following a basic guide for canning, dehydrating, and freezing foods found at the beginning of this section.

Yields: 14 pints.

Antipasto Sauce

Antipasto makes a great appetizer that is colorful and light. Always select the freshest vegetables for the best results. Omit the tuna for a great vegetarian dish.

Ingredients:

4 c. cauliflower, chopped
4 c. pearl onions
2 c. red bell peppers, chopped
2 c. yellow bell peppers, chopped
2 c. celery, chopped
2 cucumbers, peeled, seeded, chopped
2 c. carrots, chopped
2 c. olive oil
4 garlic cloves, peeled, sliced
2 c. distilled white vinegar
6 oz. canned tomato paste
1 Tbs. pickling spice, wrapped in cheesecloth
1 c. pitted black olives, halved
1½ c. pitted green olives, halved
4 c. mushrooms, canned, sliced, drained
12 oz. canned tuna, drained, and flaked
salt, to taste

Directions:

1. In large bowl, with enough lightly salted water to cover, place cauliflower, onions, red and yellow bell peppers, celery, and cucumbers.
2. Soak 8 to 12 hours, or overnight.
3. In separate bowl, place carrots with enough lightly salted water to cover.
4. Soak 8 to 12 hours, or overnight.
5. In large saucepan, place oil, garlic, vinegar, tomato paste, and cheesecloth wrapped pickling spice.
6. Bring mixture to a boil.
7. Drain and rinse the carrots.
8. Place them in the tomato paste mixture.

9. Boil 10 minutes.
10. Drain and rinse the other vegetable mixture.
11. Add them to the tomato paste and carrot mixture.
12. Cook the entire mixture 10 additional minutes, or until the cauliflower is tender, but still crisp.
13. Fold in black and green olives, mushrooms, and tuna.
14. Remove from heat.
15. Discard the wrapped pickling spice.
16. While still hot, process following a basic guide for canning, dehydrating, and freezing directions found at the beginning of this section.
17. Note: Antipasto may also be frozen in sterile, airtight containers, for up to 3 months.

Dehydrated Onions

Dehydrated onions are great to have on hand to add to your favorite recipes.

Ingredients:

onions, raw, washed

Directions:

1. Trim root and stem ends and remove paper skin.
2. Slice ⅛ to ¼-inch thick.
3. Onions may be cut into thicker pieces, but will be slightly less pungent when dried.
4. Dry at 160 degrees F. for 1 to 2 hours, and then 130 degrees F. until dry.
5. When dry, onions should feel like paper.
6. Note: Dried onions readily reabsorb moisture causing deterioration during storage.
7. Keep packaged in airtight containers in freezer, or vacuum seal.

Frozen Onions

Frozen onions are great to have on hand and may be used the same as you would a fresh onion when cooking.

Ingredients:

onions

Directions:

1. Wash, peel, and chop onions.
2. Blanch in water 2½ minutes; cool and drain.
3. Spread onions on baking sheets and place in freezer.
4. When frozen, quickly pack into moisture proof containers and place back in freezer. Plastic sealable freezer bags are great as they can be discarded after use.
5. They will keep 3 to 6 months.
6. Note: Onions may be frozen without blanching.

Dried Onions

This is a great way to store onions. It is also a fun project for kids. In recipes, replace fresh onions with half the amount of dried onions.

Ingredients:

onions, as many as desired

Directions for dehydrator or oven:

1. Peel onions.
2. Slice into ⅛-inch slices or chop into fine pieces.
3. Spread thinly over trays.
4. Dry in oven at 120 degrees F. for 24 to 30 hours, or until brittle.

5. Stir or shake onions and rotate trays every 8 hours.
6. Note: Do not mix foods in dehydrator, as flavors will blend.

Directions for sun drying:

1. Follow dehydrator steps 1 to 3.
2. Place in a well ventilated area in full sun where shade will not interrupt process.
3. Dry until papery and brittle, about 2 to 3 days.
4. Stir onions every 8 hours and take trays in at night, placing back out in the sun in the morning.

Pickled Onions

Pickling adds a completely new flavor dimension to vegetables. Try your hand at pickling today, then savor and enjoy your accomplishments later.

Ingredients:

2 med. white onions, thinly sliced
¼ c. olive oil
6 sprigs marjoram
2 bay leaves
⅛ tsp. salt
¼ c. red wine vinegar

Directions:

1. Soak onions in salted water, covered, for 10 minutes; drain.
2. Heat oil in skillet.
3. Add onions marjoram, bay leaves, and salt.
4. Cook gently over low heat until onions are tender.
5. Remove skillet from heat; stir in vinegar.
6. Serve immediately, or store in refrigerator for up to 3 days.

Zucchini Relish

This is a wonderful way to preserve some of those squash from your garden, and so handy to have on hand to use in place of the usual cucumber relish.

Ingredients:

- 6 c. zucchini, chopped
- ½ c. salt
- 6 c. water
- 2 c. onion, chopped
- ¾ c. sugar
- 2 tsp. turmeric
- 2 Tbs. celery seed
- ½ c. red bell pepper, chopped
- 1½ c. white vinegar
- ½ c. lemon juice
- 1 tsp. pepper

Directions:

1. Soak zucchini in salted water for several hours.
2. Drain and discard salt water.
3. In medium saucepan, combine zucchini, onion, sugar, turmeric, red pepper, celery seed, vinegar, and lemon juice.
4. Add pepper to taste.
5. Over medium heat, bring to boil.
6. Boil 5 minutes.
7. Process following a basic guide for canning, dehydrating, and freezing foods found at the beginning of this section.

Did You Know? . . . .

Did you know that one pound of onions contains about 175 calories?

Sweet Pickled Onions

Try these sweet pickled onions on your next appetizer tray.

Ingredients:

16 sm. boiling onions, peeled, trimmed root and stem
1½ c. malt vinegar
½ c. water
3½ Tbs. dark brown sugar, packed
2 Tbs. pickling spice
1 piece fresh ginger, (1-inch), peeled, sliced

Directions:

1. Cover onions with water in a 2 to 3-quart heavy saucepan; simmer 5 minutes.
2. Drain and transfer to clean, heatproof jar.
3. In medium saucepan, add vinegar, water, sugar, spices, and ginger; simmer 5 minutes.
4. Pour over onions to within ½-inch of jar rim.
5. Cool completely, uncovered.
6. Cover and chill for 1 week to allow flavors to develop.
7. Pickled onions can be chilled up to 3 weeks, or you can process following a basic guide for canning, dehydrating, and freezing foods found at the beginning of this section.

Yields: 2 cups.

Did You Know? . . . .

Did you know that in Rock Springs, Wyoming, a man is not allowed to chew on chunks of a raw onion while driving a pickup down the street?

Canned Onions

Canned onions make great gifts in decorative jars. Enjoy!

Ingredients:

onions, 1-inch diameter or less
water
salt

Directions:

1. Wash and peel onions.
2. Trim tops and roots flush.
3. Cover with water in saucepan and bring to a boil.
4. Boil 5 minutes and drain.
5. Pack onions into hot jars, leaving 1-inch headspace.
6. Add ½ teaspoon salt to pint jars and 1 teaspoon to quart jars, if desired.
7. Fill jar to within 1 inch from the top with boiling water.
8. Remove air bubbles.
9. Wipe jar rims and adjust lids.
10. Process both pints and quarts for 40 minutes following a basic guide for canning, dehydrating, and freezing foods found at the beginning of this section.

Did You Know? . . . .

Did you know you can reduce tears when chopping onions by cutting the bottom of a plastic bag open, and chopping inside the bag?

Did you know that munching on roasted coffee beans or sucking on a piece of cinnamon or a whole clove can neutralize onion breath?

Onion Delights Cookbook
A Collection of Onion Recipes
Cookbook Delights Series-Book 8

Salads

Table of Contents

Avocado and Onion Salad

Not only is this simple salad creamy and delicious, it is also easy to make as a last minute addition to your meal.

Ingredients:

2 lg. avocado
1 med. sweet onion, sliced into very thin rings
olive oil
salt and pepper, to taste
red pepper strips, cut very thin (optional)

Directions:

1. Carefully peel and stone each avocado.
2. Slice into thin wedges.
3. Place 4 wedges on each small serving plate.
4. Shake onion rings apart and place on top of avocado.
5. In shaker jar, add olive oil and salt and pepper to taste. Shake well.
6. When ready to serve, drizzle with the oil.
7. Add a couple strips of red pepper if desired, or use purple onions for color.

Easiest Onion Salad

This truly is the easiest onion salad to make, consisting only of fresh onions, lemon juice, salt, and black pepper.

Ingredients:

2 lg. onions, thinly sliced
2 Tbs. fresh lemon juice
½ tsp. salt
¼ tsp. black pepper

Directions:

1. In medium bowl, separate rings of onions and toss with lemon juice.
2. Add salt and pepper specified, or to taste.
3. Cover and let marinate for 1 hour; toss lightly several times.
4. Serve with main dishes, barbequed food, kabobs, or over selected greens.

Hacienda Onion Salad

The cilantro makes this delicious onion salad even better by enhancing the flavors of the onions and tomatoes.

Ingredients:

4 lg. tomatoes, cut into 8 pieces
1 lg. sweet onion, halved, thinly sliced
1 bunch fresh cilantro, chopped down to stems
1 Tbs. red wine vinegar
1 Tbs. lime juice
olive oil, to taste
salt, to taste
pepper, freshly ground, to taste
cilantro sprigs, for garnish

Directions:

1. In large salad bowl, combine tomatoes, onion, cilantro, vinegar, lime juice, and oil.
2. Toss well to blend flavors.
3. Add salt and freshly ground pepper to taste; toss lightly.
4. Cover and refrigerate for several hours.
5. When ready to serve, garnish with cilantro sprigs.

Maitake Mushroom and Spinach Salad

This is a great salad, and as the Germans say, "Es gibt nichts besserer als frischer Zwiebelsalat im Sommer." "There is nothing better than fresh onion salad in the summer."

Ingredients:

3½ oz. Maitake mushrooms
1 cube chicken bouillon
1 c. water
7 oz. boneless chicken breast, cut into ½-inch strips
2 med. onions, sliced, rinsed
1 bunch spinach, rinsed, stems removed
4 Tbs. mustard
4 Tbs. Italian dressing
4 lg. radishes, washed, topped, sliced, for garnish
salt and fresh ground pepper, to taste

Directions:

1. Break mushrooms into bite-size pieces.
2. In medium saucepan, bring 1 cup water to boil.
3. Add bouillon cube.
4. Add chicken and mushrooms to bouillon.
5. Heat until chicken is cooked; drain and cool.
6. Blot excess water from onion and spinach; place in large salad bowl.
7. Add mushrooms and chicken on top of spinach and onion.
8. Cover; chill 2 hours in refrigerator.
9. In shaker jar, add mustard, Italian dressing, salt and pepper to taste; shake well to blend.
10. When ready to serve, pour dressing over salad and garnish with radishes.

Summer Salad

This is a healthy, delicious salad. Add soup as well for a filling meal.

Ingredients for salad:

1 can kidney beans, drained, rinsed
1 can black beans, drained, rinsed
3 sm. potatoes, boiled, sliced
1 lg. sweet onion, peeled, chopped
1 c. celery, chopped
2 lg. Roma tomatoes, cut into sm. pieces
1 tsp. garlic, chopped
1 lg. head lettuce, washed, torn in chunks
salt and pepper, to taste

Ingredients for dressing:

2 Tbs. olive oil
2 tsp. safflower oil
4 tsp. lemon juice
4 Tbs. malt vinegar

Directions for salad and dressing:

1. In large mixing bowl, combine beans, potatoes, onion, celery, tomatoes, and garlic.
2. Season with salt and pepper to taste.
3. Place lettuce in a large glass salad bowl and make a well in the center.
4. Place combined vegetables in center of bowl.
5. In small bowl, stir together oils, lemon juice, and vinegar. Sprinkle over top of vegetables.
6. Reserve some dressing in a small bowl and place on the table for guests to add more if desired.
7. Note: This may be covered and refrigerated for 2 hours before serving if necessary.

Broccoli Salad with Red Onion and Bacon

I love bacon, and combined with red onions and raisins, this broccoli salad is absolutely delicious!

Ingredients:

8 slices bacon, cooked, crumbled
2 c. broccoli, chopped into bite-size pieces
½ c. red onion, chopped
⅓ c. raisins
⅓ c. sunflower seeds
1 c. mayonnaise
2 Tbs. sugar
2 Tbs. lemon juice
salt and pepper, to taste
milk, for thinning if necessary

Directions:

1. In small skillet, fry bacon until crisp.
2. Cool and crumble; set aside.
3. In large bowl, combine broccoli, onions, raisins, and sunflower seeds; set aside.
4. In small bowl or shaker jar, combine mayonnaise, sugar, lemon juice, salt, and pepper.
5. Dilute dressing with a tablespoon of milk if too thick.
6. Pour dressing over salad mixture.
7. Cover and refrigerate until ready to serve.
8. When ready to serve, add bacon and toss lightly.

Did You Know? . . . .

Did you know the skins of two red onions or yellow storage onions are enough to dye one dozen eggs?

Onion, Potato, and Apple Salad

This makes a flavorful potato salad. It is one of those dishes that always seems to be even better the following day, so don't hesitate to make this the day before it will be served.

Ingredients:

6 lg. red potatoes, peeled, cooked
1 lg. sweet Bermuda, Vidalia, or Walla Walla onion
¾ c. celery, sliced
1 lg. Golden Delicious apple, diced
20 lg. pimento stuffed olives, sliced
⅓ c. sweet pickle or zucchini relish
1½ c. mayonnaise
1 tsp. celery seed
2 tsp. Dijon mustard
2 Tbs. white wine vinegar
salt and pepper, to taste

Directions:

1. In large bowl, cube potatoes.
2. Slice onions into 4 pieces and then into thin slices vertically.
3. In small bowl, combine onions, celery, apples, olives, and relish.
4. Add to potatoes, mix lightly.
5. In another small bowl, stir together mayonnaise, celery seed, vinegar, mustard; and salt and pepper to taste.
6. Drizzle carefully over potatoes.
7. Toss gently to avoid breaking up potatoes.
8. Cover.
9. Refrigerate several hours or overnight to blend flavors before serving.

Tomato and Onion Salad

Fresh tomatoes and sweet onion slices make a great salad by themselves, or you can add them to greens.

Ingredients:

1 firm tomato
1 med. Walla Walla sweet onion
dressing of your choice

Directions:

1. Cut tomatoes into ¼-inch slices.
2. Thinly slice onion and place alternately in salad bowl with tomatoes.
3. Pour dressing over top.
4. Cover and refrigerate to let tomatoes and onions marinate.
5. When ready to serve, they can be served just the way they are, or a suggestion of being added to a select greens salad with halved boiled eggs on the side.

Chickpea, Pesto, and Red Onion Salad

This simple salad is both easy to make and delicious. It is a quick and elegant salad for company when you need one in a hurry.

Ingredients:

2 c. canned chickpeas
3 Tbs. ready-made pesto sauce
1 Tbs. olive oil
1 Tbs. lemon juice
¾ c. red onions, chopped

Directions:

1. Drain and rinse chickpeas.
2. In medium bowl, whisk pesto, oil, and lemon juice together.
3. Add chickpeas and red onions; toss lightly.
4. This salad is best served at room temperature.

Onion Potato Salad

Red potatoes have great flavor and so do Walla Walla Sweet Onions. Add dill pickles, green olives, and Dijon mustard, and you have a fantastic potato salad.

Ingredients:

3 lb. red potatoes, peeled, cooked
1 lg. Walla Walla onion, peeled
1 c. celery, sliced
20 lg. pimento stuffed olives, sliced
⅓ c. pickle relish
1½ c. mayonnaise
2 Tbs. white wine vinegar
2 tsp. Dijon mustard
salt and pepper, to taste

Directions:

1. Cube potatoes; slice onions into thin slices.
2. In large bowl, combine potatoes, onions, celery, olives, and pickle relish.
3. In small bowl, blend mayonnaise, vinegar, and mustard well.
4. Pour over potatoes and lightly combine so as not to break up potatoes.
5. Season with salt and pepper to taste.
6. Cover; refrigerate several hours or overnight to blend flavors before serving.

German Potato Salad

We have always found this German style salad excellent for picnics and summer dinners. It is such a change of pace, as it is served warm and needs no refrigeration.

Ingredients:

6 lg. potatoes, unpeeled, boiled, chopped
1 Vidalia sweet onion, peeled, chopped
3 eggs, hard-boiled, chopped
¾ lb. bacon, fried crisp, crumpled, reserve drippings
½ tsp. celery salt
⅓ c. sugar
salt and pepper, to taste
tarragon vinegar, equal to the amount of bacon drippings

Directions:

1. In medium bowl, combine potatoes, onions, and eggs.
2. Sprinkle with salt, pepper, and celery salt; set aside.
3. In small pan, measure bacon drippings and bring to a boil.
4. Add equal amount of tarragon vinegar, and sugar.
5. Boil for 1 minute.
6. Pour over potato mix.
7. Taste and adjust seasonings if necessary.
8. Crumble bacon and add to mixture.
9. Toss lightly; serve warm or at room temperature.

Did You Know? . . . .

Did you know that many people will not like it when they visit Wade Mills, North Carolina? Neither onions nor ice cream can be purchased or eaten on Sunday during the half hour period before a church starts its services.

Layered Onion Salad

Bacon and Swiss cheese make this layered onion salad one to savor with the delicate blend of flavors.

Ingredients:

- 2 med. red onions, thinly sliced
- 1 head iceberg lettuce, torn into chunks
- ¾ c. mayonnaise
- 2 Tbs. milk
- 2 tsp. sugar
- 10 oz. frozen peas
- 1 c. Swiss cheese, diced
- 3 slices bacon, cooked, crumbled
- ½ tsp. salt
- ⅛ tsp. black pepper

Directions:

1. Separate onions into rings.
2. Place in cold water for 1 hour; drain.
3. In small bowl, mix mayonnaise with milk.
4. Pour half of the mixture over top of the lettuce.
5. Add a layer of ⅓ onions.
6. Sprinkle with half the sugar, half the peas, half of the cheeses, and half of the salt and pepper.
7. Repeat layers again in same order.
8. Top with final ⅓ of onion rings.
9. Cover.
10. Refrigerate 1 to 2 hours before serving.
11. When ready to serve, sprinkle the crumbled bacon over the top.

Did You Know? . . . .

Did you know that the official state vegetable of Georgia is the Vidalia onion?

Orange, Vidalia Sweet Onion Salad

Orange slices are delicious with the Vidalia sweet onions. Enjoy this salad with your favorite main dish.

Ingredients for salad:

8 oranges, peeled, sectioned, cut into pieces
2 med. Vidalia sweet onions, peeled, sliced
3 c. lettuce, shredded

Ingredients for dressing:

6 Tbs. olive oil
3 Tbs. apple cider vinegar
3 Tbs. honey
½ c. garlic cloves, crushed
1 Tbs. celery seed
1 Tbs. basil
1 tsp. oregano

Directions for dressing and salad:

1. In small bowl, combine oil, vinegar, and honey; mix well.
2. Add garlic, celery seed, basil, and oregano together.
3. Blend thoroughly.
4. In a salad bowl, combine oranges and onions.
5. Add dressing and toss well.
6. Cover.
7. Refrigerate several hours to blend flavors.
8. When ready to serve, put shredded lettuce on individual serving dishes.
9. Spoon salad on top of lettuce.

Yields: 6 servings.

Radish, Apple, and Onion Salad

Red radishes, red apples, and red onions make a delicious and colorful salad.

Ingredients for salad:

2 Red Delicious apples, cored, seeded, thinly sliced
2 tsp. lemon juice
½ red onion, peeled, thinly sliced
4 radishes, washed, trimmed, thinly sliced
1 head romaine lettuce or red leaf lettuce, chopped

Ingredients for dressing:

3 Tbs. red wine vinegar
2 tsp. sugar
1 tsp. salt
¼ c. extra virgin olive oil
½ c. sour cream
1 tsp. poppy seeds
2 Tbs. dill, chopped, or 2 tsp. dried dill

Directions for salad and dressing:

1. In large salad bowl, combine apples with lemon juice to impede browning.
2. Add onion and radishes.
3. Toss all together with chopped lettuce.
4. In small bowl, combine vinegar, sugar, and salt.
5. Whisk in oil.
6. Stir in sour cream, poppy seeds, and dill.
7. Drizzle dressing evenly over salad.
8. Serve with your favorite main dish or soup.

Yields: 4 servings.

Spinach and Red Onion Salad

Spinach and red onions combine to make a very flavorful and healthy salad.

Ingredients for dressing:

¼ c. red wine vinegar
½ c. extra virgin olive oil
black pepper, freshly ground, to taste
garlic croutons

Ingredients for salad:

1 med. red onion, thinly sliced
fresh spinach leaves, washed and spun dry
Parmesan cheese, freshly grated

Directions for dressing and salad:

1. In small bowl, mix together vinegar and oil.
2. Place spinach leaves on individual serving plates.
3. Top with onions, cheese, and fresh pepper.
4. When ready to serve, pour dressing over the top.
5. Sprinkle with croutons.

Yields: 4 servings.

Did You Know? . . . .

Did you know that if you are an onion-loving male stopping over in Headland, Alabama, you need to be on guard? If going out on the town in an effort to meet one of the local cuties, there is an old piece of legalese that says, "No man can place his arm around or kiss an unchaperoned woman without a good and lawful reason," should he have eaten onions within the last hours.

Onion Delights Cookbook
A Collection of Onion Recipes
Cookbook Delights Series-Book 8

Side Dishes

Table of Contents

Capellini with Caramelized Onions and Cheese

When fried in butter and olive oil, cooked pasta becomes crisp and delicious. This golden cake, flavored with Parmesan and parsley, is a great side dish alternative to potatoes or rice.

Ingredients:

2 Tbs. butter, divided
2 Tbs. olive oil, divided
3 onions, sliced
1½ tsp. salt, divided
½ lb. capellini or angel hair pasta
2 eggs
¾ c. Parmesan cheese, grated
¼ c. fresh parsley, chopped
¼ tsp. black pepper, fresh ground

Directions:

1. In large frying pan, over low heat, melt 1 tablespoon of butter with 1 tablespoon oil.
2. Add onions and ½ teaspoon of the salt.
3. Cover; cook onions until very soft, 20 minutes.
4. Uncover onions; increase heat to medium-high, and cook, stirring frequently, until onions are golden brown, 10 minutes.
5. In large pot of boiling, salted water, cook pasta until just done, 3 minutes; drain and rinse.
6. Transfer pasta to large bowl and let cool slightly.
7. Beat eggs and add to pasta along with onions, cheese, parsley, remaining 1 teaspoon salt, and pepper; mix well to coat pasta.
8. In a 12-inch nonstick frying pan, over moderately low heat, melt ½ tablespoon of the butter with ½ tablespoon oil.

9. Add capellini mixture and press down to form flat cake
10. Cook 15 minutes, or until crisp golden crust forms on bottom.
11. Place large platter or baking sheet over pan.
12. Invert pan so cake drops out.
13. In skillet, over medium heat, melt remaining ½ tablespoon butter with remaining ½ tablespoon oil.
14. Slide cake back into pan and cook 5 minutes, until golden crust forms on other side.
15. Cut into wedges and serve at once.

Baked Onions

This is a nice side dish to accompany roast beef, roasted pork, or poultry main dish.

Ingredients:

- 2 lg. yellow or white onions, peeled
- 2 Tbs. tomato juice
- 1½ Tbs. honey
- 1 Tbs. butter
- ½ tsp. salt
- ⅛ tsp. paprika
- canola oil

Directions:

1. Preheat oven to 350 degrees F.
2. Cut onions in half crosswise, and place cut side up, in a lightly oiled baking dish.
3. In small saucepan, over low heat, combine tomato juice, honey, and butter until butter is melted; stir well.
4. Pour over center of each onion half; season with salt and paprika.
5. Cover and bake 40 to 45 minutes.
6. Remove from oven and serve while warm.

Lemon Noodles

Lemon butter sauce is a refreshing citrus addition to spaghetti, and the onions add even more delectable flavors.

Ingredients:

1 lb. noodles, thin type
½ c. butter
1 med. onion, chopped
2 c. sour cream
1 tsp. lemon peel, grated
¼ c. parsley, minced
¼ c. bread crumbs, finely crushed
Parmesan cheese, to taste
juice of 1 or 2 lemons
freshly ground pepper, to taste

Directions:

1. Preheat oven to 400 degrees F.
2. Lightly butter a casserole dish.
3. Cook noodles as directed on package; drain and set aside.
4. Melt butter in a saucepan; add chopped onions and sauté until tender. Remove from heat.
5. Stir in sour cream, lemon juice, and lemon peel.
6. Add noodles, Parmesan cheese, salt and pepper to taste; toss to coat well.
7. Place mixture into prepared dish; sprinkle parsley and bread crumbs over top.
8. Bake 20 to 25 minutes.
9. Remove from oven and serve while hot.

Did You Know? . . . .

Did you know in Callicoon, New York, it is against the law to sell onions and ice cream sodas on Sunday?

Lentils and Rice Surprise

This is a delicious dish that can be made ahead of time and cooked when cold. This recipe is really handy when you are short on time; just add 15 minutes to oven cooking time.

Ingredients:

1 c. lentils, dried
1 med. onion
⅓ c. water
1 garlic clove, chopped
3 celery stalks, chopped
1 can tomato sauce (28 oz.)
1 tsp. dill weed
3 c. rice, cooked
1 c. bread crumbs

Directions:

1. In medium saucepan, add lentils and water to cover; bring to boil.
2. Cover; simmer over low heat 1½ hours, until tender.
3. Drain liquid reserving ½ cup.
4. In large pot, heat ⅓ cup water.
5. Add onion, garlic, and celery; cook over medium heat for 15 minutes.
6. Add tomato sauce, drained lentils with ½ cup reserved liquid, rice, and dill weed; mix well.
7. Grease a 3-quart casserole.
8. Sprinkle a few bread crumbs over the bottom.
9. Pour lentil-rice mixture into the casserole.
10. Sprinkle the rest of the crumbs over the top.
11. Bake in preheated oven at 350 degrees F. for 45 minutes.
12. Serve while hot.

Mashed Potatoes with Onion Bits

These mashed, red potatoes are cooked with the skins on for the added flavor, texture, and vitamins. Adding the onion gives them an "out of the ordinary" taste.

Ingredients:

1 sm. onion, peeled, diced
1 Tbs. olive oil
12 med. red potatoes, washed, leave skins on
⅔ c. milk
½ c. butter, softened
1 tsp. salt
½ tsp. pepper
paprika, for garnish

Directions:

1. In small saucepan, place onion and oil.
2. Sauté onion just until soft, but not browned.
3. Place potatoes in 6-quart or larger kettle.
4. Add enough water to cover potatoes.
5. Heat to boiling; reduce heat.
6. Cover and simmer 20 to 30 minutes, or until potatoes are tender; drain.
7. Shake pan with potatoes over low heat to dry. This will make the mashed potatoes fluffier.
8. Add butter, salt, pepper, and milk.
9. Mash vigorously until potatoes are light and fluffy.
10. Sprinkle onions over mashed potatoes.
11. Stir just enough to incorporate them.
12. Place in serving bowl.
13. Top with dots of butter and a shake or two of paprika for garnish.

Yields: 8 to 10 servings.

Mushroom and Chive Pilaf

This makes a great side dish with seafood. Our family loves rice and this is an easy-to-make dish.

Ingredients:

1 Tbs. olive oil
½ c. fresh onion, minced
1 garlic clove, minced
2 c. chicken broth
½ tsp. white pepper
1 c. basmati rice, uncooked
8 oz. fresh mushrooms, chopped
1 c. chives, chopped
¼ c. green onions, thinly sliced
salt, to taste (optional)

Directions:

1. In medium saucepan, over medium-high heat, heat oil.
2. Add onion and garlic.
3. Sauté 2 minutes.
4. Add broth, salt, if desired, and pepper.
5. Bring to boil; stir in rice and mushrooms.
6. Cover and reduce heat; simmer 35 minutes.
7. Remove from heat.
8. Let stand 5 minutes to absorb liquid.
9. Stir in the chives.
10. When ready to serve, place in serving bowl and sprinkle green onions over the top.

Did You Know? . . . .

Did you know you can reduce tears when chopping onions by using a sharp knife, so the chopping goes faster, or by chilling the onion first?

Southwestern Noodles and Onions

Corn is one of the old staples in the southwest diet. This is a delicious side dish, and so easy to make.

Ingredients:

4 oz. med. egg noodles
1 c. frozen corn
1 c. green onions, sliced
½ c. salsa
2 c. tomato sauce
1 c. water
¼ c. cheese, shredded

Directions:

1. In medium saucepan, heat water to boiling; add the noodles.
2. Reduce heat to low; cover and simmer 10 to 12 minutes. Drain.
3. Add corn, onions, salsa, tomato sauce, and water.
4. Bring to boil; reduce and simmer until liquid is almost gone.
5. Remove from heat and place in serving bowl.
6. Sprinkle with cheese and serve.

Zucchini, Bacon, and Onion Side Dish

A rich blend of onions, zucchini, and bacon in a cheese sauce makes this side dish a welcome addition to your meal.

Ingredients:

1 med. onion, diced
5 slices bacon, diced
3 med. zucchini, angle sliced ¼-inch thick
½ c. cream
2 Tbs. Parmesan cheese, freshly grated
1½ Tbs. dried basil

Directions:

1. Dice bacon and onion.
2. Place together in a two-handle skillet over medium-high heat; sauté until golden.
3. Turn heat down to simmer; layer zucchini on top of onion and bacon.
4. Cook, covered for 8 minutes, or just until squash is tender.
5. In small bowl, mix cream, Parmesan cheese, and basil together.
6. Pour over zucchini, bacon, and onion as it is cooking.
7. Cover and cook for another 2 minutes.
8. Remove from heat; serve in the skillet while hot.

Pearl Baked Cream Onions

This is a delicious side dish to complement any meat, poultry, pork, or fish.

Ingredients:

4 c. pearl onions
½ tsp. salt
½ tsp. pepper
⅓ c. butter, melted
2½ c. buttery round crackers, crushed
1⅓ c. heavy cream

Directions:

1. Preheat oven to 350 degrees F.
2. Place onions in a 2-quart casserole dish.
3. Season with salt and pepper.
4. Pour melted butter over onions.
5. Sprinkle crushed crackers on top.
6. Pour cream over crackers.
7. Bake 50 minutes.

Onion Bread Pudding

This is a tasty side dish or appetizer and a delicious alternative to potatoes.

Ingredients:

1 Tbs. butter
1 Tbs. canola oil
1½ c. sweet onion, finely chopped
4 slices bread, stale
1 c. milk
¼ c. cream
2 c. eggs
1 tsp. hot sauce
2 Tbs. fresh parsley, chopped
1 tsp. sesame seeds, toasted
salt and freshly ground pepper, to taste

Directions:

1. Preheat oven to 350 degrees F.
2. Lightly butter a 1½-quart casserole dish.
3. In large skillet, melt butter with oil.
4. Add onion slowly; sauté over low heat until tender and golden, but not browned; about 30 minutes, then set aside.
5. Butter each bread slice lightly on both sides.
6. Cut into cubes and spread half over the bottom of prepared dish.
7. Sprinkle with cooked onions and top with remaining bread cubes.
8. In small bowl, whisk together milk, cream, eggs, hot sauce, parsley, and salt and pepper to taste.
9. Pour over bread mixture.
10. Sprinkle the toasted sesame seeds evenly over the top.
11. Bake 45 to 50 minutes, or until the pudding is fluffy and the top crispy golden.

Zesty Mexican Rice

This is a tasty Mexican-style rice and additionally delicious when it is reheated.

Ingredients:

2	Tbs. canola oil
1	c. brown rice, uncooked
1	c. tomatoes, chopped
2	Tbs. tomato sauce
1	sm. onion, chopped
2	garlic cloves, minced
2⅓	c. vegetarian stock
1	c. carrots, cooked, diced
½	c. peas, cooked
1	Tbs. green chilies, chopped
1	Tbs. fresh parsley, chopped

Directions:

1. In large saucepan, heat oil.
2. Add rice and stir until coated with the oil; set aside.
3. In blender, purée tomatoes, tomato sauce, onion, garlic and ⅓ cup of the vegetable stock, until smooth.
4. Pour this mixture and the remainder of the stock into the saucepan holding the rice.
5. Cover.
6. Cook, over medium heat, 45 minutes or until liquid has been absorbed and rice is tender.
7. Stir in carrots, peas, chilies, and parsley.
8. Heat through.
9. Serve immediately.
10. Note: You may cool and refrigerate for 1 to 2 days.
11. Reheat in a saucepan or ovenproof casserole at 350 degrees F. for 30 minutes.

Stuffed Marrow Squash

This is a traditional squash found in Ireland, and it can be substituted with a butternut, Hubbard, or any hard-skinned winter-type squash if a marrow squash is not available in your area.

Ingredients:

- 8 oz. cooked lamb, chopped well
- 1 onion, finely chopped
- 1 carrot, finely chopped
- 1 c. gravy or stock made with bouillon cube
- 3 lg. tomatoes
- 1½ c. rice, cooked
- ½ tsp. oregano
- ½ c. mixed garden herbs, chopped
- 1 lg. marrow squash
- salt and pepper, to taste

Directions:

1. Preheat oven to 400 degrees F.
2. Put lamb, onion, and carrot through the grinder or chop in food processor.
3. Combine in bowl with gravy or stock.
4. Place tomatoes in boiling water for a few minutes; lift out and remove skins.
5. Chop and add to mixture.
6. Add rice and herbs; season with salt and pepper, to taste.
7. Scrub squash well; cut in half lengthwise; remove seeds.
8. Fill both halves with stuffing.
9. Place side by side in pan with ½ inch of water in bottom.
10. Cover with foil.
11. Bake for 1 hour.

12. Remove from oven and lift off foil.
13. Sprinkle grated cheese over tops of squash and return to oven for 10 minutes.
14. Remove from oven; serve while hot.

Tasty Barbequed Lentils

Here is a wonderful way to serve those favorite lentils. The barbeque sauce gives it a wonderful zest!

Ingredients:

2⅓ c. lentils, rinsed
5 c. water
½ c. molasses
2 Tbs. brown sugar
1 Tbs. vinegar
½ c. ketchup
1 tsp. dry mustard
1 tsp. hot sauce
1 can tomato sauce (16 oz.)
2 Tbs. minced onions
butter

Directions:

1. In medium saucepan, bring water to boil, add lentils; simmer 30 minutes, or until tender but remain whole; drain.
2. Add molasses, brown sugar, vinegar, ketchup, and dry mustard; blend well.
3. Stir in hot sauce, tomato sauce, and minced onions; place in buttered casserole dish.
4. Bake in preheated oven at 350 degrees F. for 45 minutes.
5. Remove from oven; serve either hot or cool to room temperature for picnic style.

Wild Rice with Snow Peas

This is another flavored wild rice recipe with lots of interesting textures. It can easily be made with vegetable broth for vegetarians.

Ingredients:

1 c. wild rice
4 scallions, washed, outer skin and roots removed
2 Tbs. butter
1 tsp. salt
2 c. or more chicken broth
2 Tbs. olive oil
1 c. snow peas, sliced
8 lg. mushrooms, thinly sliced
1 sm. can water chestnuts, drained, thinly sliced
¾ c. toasted almonds
salt
freshly ground black pepper

Directions:

1. Rinse rice thoroughly, several times.
2. Cut green scallion stems diagonally into 2-inch lengths; finely chop the white part.
3. In large saucepan, melt butter.
4. Sauté minced white scallion until tender.
5. Add rice, salt, and chicken broth.
6. Bring to boil; stir once and reduce heat.
7. Cover tightly and cook over low heat until rice is tender and liquid is absorbed; 35 minutes.
8. If necessary, add more broth as rice cooks.
9. While rice is cooking, remove ends and strings from peas; slice diagonally and measure 1 cup.
10. Heat oil in large skillet.
11. Add scallion stems, peas, mushrooms, water chestnuts, and almonds.

12. Sauté only until mushrooms are tender.
13. Combine the cooked rice and vegetable mixture.
14. Add salt and pepper to taste.
15. Place in a lightly buttered casserole dish and sprinkle with toasted almonds.
16. Cover and keep hot in a very slow oven until serving.

Sweet Potato Cakes

These sweet potato cakes are delicious. Take them on a picnic or to a potluck dinner.

Ingredients:

1 lg. sweet potato, grated
1½ oz. sweet onion, grated
2 Tbs. green onion, chopped
1 egg
½ oz. flour
¾ tsp. salt
1 dash white pepper
1 c. canola oil
½ tsp. lemon juice
1 tsp. parsley, chopped
sour cream
canola oil

Directions:

1. In large mixing bowl, combine potato, onions, egg, and flour; adjust salt and pepper to taste.
2. Form into three 4-inch patties.
3. In large skillet, on medium heat, heat oil. Pan-fry patties until lightly browned and heated thoroughly.
4. When ready to serve, top with sour cream that has been blended with lemon juice, and sprinkle the parsley over each serving.

Scalloped Cabbage

This cabbage casserole is delicious. It is great served with ham, pork, fish, or any barbequed meat.

Ingredients:

- 2 Tbs. butter, divided
- 1 med. head cabbage, cored, thinly sliced
- 1 lg. onion, chopped
- 1½ c. milk
- 4 eggs, lightly beaten
- 1 c. saltine crackers, crushed, divided
- 1 tsp. salt
- ½ tsp. ground black pepper

Directions:

1. Preheat oven to 350 degrees F.
2. Grease a 9 x12-inch casserole dish.
3. In a large pot, over medium heat, melt 1 tablespoon of butter.
4. Add cabbage and onion.
5. Cook 20 minutes, or until tender, stirring often.
6. Add milk and bring to a boil.
7. Reduce heat to low.
8. Simmer for 5 minutes.
9. Gently pour in eggs, stirring constantly.
10. Stir in ¾ of the cracker crumbs and salt and pepper; mix well.
11. Pour into casserole dish.
12. Top with remaining cracker crumbs.
13. Dot with remaining butter.
14. Bake 30 minutes, or until golden brown and heated through.

Onion Delights Cookbook
A Collection of Onion Recipes
Cookbook Delights Series-Book 8

Soups

Table of Contents

African Peanut Onion Soup

This is a thick, hearty soup that is delicious. Serve it topped with plenty of chopped scallions and chopped peanuts.

Ingredients:

2 c. onion, chopped
1 Tbs. canola oil
½ tsp. cayenne pepper
1 tsp. fresh ginger, peeled, grated
1 c. carrots, chopped
4 c. vegetable stock or water
2 c. sweet potatoes, chopped
2 c. tomato juice
1 c. smooth peanut butter
1 Tbs. sugar
¼ c. scallions, chopped
½ c. peanuts, roasted, chopped

Directions:

1. In skillet, over medium-high heat, sauté onion in oil until it is translucent.
2. Stir in cayenne and ginger.
3. Add carrots and sauté 2 to 3 minutes more.
4. Stir in the stock; add potatoes and bring to boil.
5. Reduce heat to simmer; cook 15 minutes, or until vegetables are tender.
6. Remove from heat; scoop vegetables out and place in blender with tomato juice.
7. Purée, adding cooking liquid if necessary.
8. Return purée to pot.
9. Add peanut butter and stir until smooth.
10. Check sweetness and add sugar if necessary.
11. Reheat gently if necessary on simmer, or in microwave to prevent scorching.
12. Add more water, stock, or tomato juice to make a thinner soup if desired.

13. Ladle into individual bowls and top with chopped peanuts and scallions.

Beef Onion Soup

This is a very easy-to-make and healthy soup that tastes great. Our family loves it served with homemade noodles, pastry, or dumplings.

Ingredients:

- 1 lb. stew beef, cut into sm. pieces
- 1 Tbs. canola oil
- 4 c. beef broth
- 1 med. onion, chopped
- 3 c. water
- 1 can tomatoes, crushed (14 oz.)
- 1½ c. potatoes, cubed
- 1 c. carrots, sliced
- 1 c. celery, sliced
- ½ c. frozen corn
- 1 c. frozen green beans
- 1 tsp. basil, oregano, dill, or combination
- ½ c. frozen peas

Directions:

1. In large pot, over medium-high heat, brown beef pieces in oil.
2. Add beef broth and onions, cook 3 minutes longer.
3. Add water and tomatoes; cook until beef is tender.
4. Increase heat to medium.
5. Add potatoes, carrots, celery, corn, and green beans.
6. Cook until vegetables are tender.
7. Add spices and peas, mix well.
8. Reduce heat; simmer another 30 minutes.
9. Note: At this stage you can add noodles, or make dumplings to top off soup.
10. Serve with your favorite crackers or bread.

Black Bean Onion Soup

My husband especially loves black bean soup. This soup is rich and full of flavor, especially with the Cheddar cheese.

Ingredients:

2 med. onions, chopped
2 garlic cloves, minced
1 Tbs. canola oil
6 c. black beans, cooked
7 c. water
1½ c. green pepper, chopped
salt and pepper, to taste
sharp Cheddar cheese, shredded, to taste
whole wheat bread or crackers

Directions:

1. In a skillet, over medium heat, sauté onion and garlic in oil for 5 to 7 minutes, or until soft.
2. In large pot, add beans and water.
3. Add garlic and onion mixture; bring to a boil.
4. Add green pepper.
5. Reduce heat; simmer 10 minutes.
6. Remove from heat and cool slightly.
7. Scoop out half of soup ingredients and purée in a blender.
8. Return purée to pot.
9. Add salt and pepper to taste.
10. Reheat to serving temperature.
11. When ready to serve, ladle into individual bowls and top with cheese.
12. Serve with some of your homemade crackers or whole wheat bread for a meal in itself.

Caramelized Onion Soup

The caramelized onions are delicious and add great flavor to this soup.

Ingredients:

4 lb. onions, peeled, sliced
2 Tbs. butter, melted
2 Tbs. olive oil
1½ tsp. kosher salt
2 Tbs. flour
1 Tbs. brown sugar
3 c. chicken stock, hot
3 c. beef stock, hot
2 Tbs. port wine

Directions:

1. In crockpot, combine onions, butter, olive oil, and salt.
2. Cover; cook on high for 1 hour.
3. Reduce heat to low; stir every hour so onions color evenly.
4. Cook 5 to 6 hours, until onions are nicely browned or caramelized.
5. When onions are done, sprinkle in the flour and sugar. Stir gently to incorporate.
6. Cook on low heat, 30 minutes, stirring occasionally.
7. Add all of the hot stock.
8. Return heat to high and cook 1 hour.
9. Reduce heat to low; cook 2 hours longer; then stir in wine.
10. When ready to serve, ladle into individual bowls.
11. Add slices of toasted French bread.
12. Top with melted Parmesan cheese on the side.

Cheesy Onion Soup

This creamy, cheesy onion soup is delicious and tastes best when it is made with Colby or sharp Cheddar cheese.

Ingredients:

3 Tbs. butter
4 onions, diced
3 Tbs. flour
1 qt. milk
1 c. Colby cheese, grated
salt and pepper, to taste
paprika, to garnish

Directions:

1. In large pot, melt butter.
2. Add onions and sauté until browned.
3. Add flour, stirring constantly for 2 minutes.
4. Continuing to stir, add milk a little at a time.
5. When soup has thickened, turn heat to simmer and add cheese.
6. Stir until cheese has melted and soup is smooth.
7. Season to taste with salt and pepper.
8. When ready to serve, ladle soup into bowls.
9. Sprinkle with paprika and serve.
10. Try some crusty bread on the side and perhaps a salad to make a wholesome meal.

Did You Know?. . . .

Did you know that it is against the law in Okanogan, Washington, to eat onions in public with a spoon?

Corned Beef, Onion, and Barley Soup

This is a delicious soup that comes from Ireland. It is fairly easy to make, and it is a meal in itself.

Ingredients:

3 lb. corned beef brisket, cubed
4 Tbs. olive oil
2 qt. beef broth
1 tsp. oregano
1 tsp. basil
½ tsp. thyme
1 bunch parsley, chopped
2 med. onions, chopped
2 celery ribs, chopped
2 carrots, chopped
1 c. pearl barley
4 c. canned tomatoes, diced or chopped

Directions:

1. In Dutch oven, heat oil.
2. Add corned beef and brown thoroughly.
3. Stir in broth, oregano, basil, thyme, and parsley.
4. Bring mixture to a boil.
5. Add onions, celery, carrots, and barley.
6. Reduce heat and simmer 1 hour.
7. Stir in tomatoes; simmer 30 minutes more.
8. Add salt and freshly ground black pepper, to taste.
9. When ready to serve, ladle into warmed bowls.
10. Serve with crusty bread, or homemade scones on the side.

Did You Know? . . . .

Did you know in Hartsburg, Illinois, it is illegal to take onions to the local movie theater as a snack?

Cream of Leek Soup with Stilton Cheese

The addition of nutmeg puts a new twist on this great cream soup as a companion to your meal or a meal in its own.

Ingredients:

1 Tbs. butter
1 Tbs. shallots, finely chopped
2 c. leeks, coarsely chopped
½ c. raw potato, cubed
2 c. chicken stock, heated
1½ c. whipping or heavy cream
2 oz. Stilton cheese, crumbled
salt and pepper, to taste
nutmeg, to taste
lemon juice, to taste

Directions:

1. In large pot, sauté shallots and leeks in butter until transparent.
2. Add potato and chicken stock.
3. Cook 20 minutes.
4. Cool 10 minutes.
5. Pour contents into a blender container.
6. Purée until smooth.
7. In medium saucepan, over medium heat, heat whipping cream with nutmeg and lemon juice.
8. Add to potato mixture.
9. Add salt and pepper to taste.
10. When ready to serve, heat through and ladle into individual serving bowls.
11. Sprinkle crumbled cheese over the top.
12. Add a slice of garlic bread on the side.

Creamy Onion Soup

This creamy onion soup has great flavor and is easy to make.

Ingredients:

- ⅓ c. butter
- 5 lg. onions, peeled, quartered
- 5 c. beef broth
- ½ c. dried celery leaves or dried celery flakes
- 1 lg. potato, peeled, quartered
- 1¼ c. white port or cream sherry
- ¾ c. vinegar, or more if desired
- 4 Tbs. sugar
- 1 c. heavy whipping cream
- 1 Tbs. dried parsley flakes
- salt and pepper, to taste

Directions:

1. In large pot, melt butter; sauté onions to bring out the flavor and sweetness.
2. Add beef broth, celery leaves or flakes, potatoes, and bring to boil.
3. Cover pot; simmer on medium heat for 30 minutes.
4. Remove from heat and cool.
5. Scoop ingredients from broth; purée in 2 or 3 batches in blender.
6. Place purée back into the pot of broth.
7. Add wine, vinegar, and sugar; blend well.
8. Return to heat and bring to boil again.
9. Reduce heat to low; simmer 5 minutes.
10. Stir cream and parsley in well; salt and pepper to taste.
11. Continue to simmer another 5 minutes, being careful not to boil.
12. When ready to serve, ladle into individual bowls and top with a sprinkle of celery or parsley leaves.

Creamy Vidalia Onion Chowder

This creamy onion and corn chowder has a delicious taste with the added flavors of bacon and cream.

Ingredients:

- 8 slices bacon
- 3 Tbs. olive oil
- 4 med. Vidalia or a sweet onion, peeled, chopped
- 1 Tbs. garlic, minced
- 2 cans chicken broth (14½ oz. ea.)
- 2½ c. potatoes, mashed
- 2 c. frozen corn
- 2 bay leaves
- ¼ tsp. dried thyme
- ¾ c. sour cream
- ground black pepper, to taste
- salt, to taste

Directions:

1. In skillet, place bacon; fry until crisp.
2. Remove and blot with paper towel to remove excess grease; cool, coarsely chop and set aside.
3. In Dutch oven, over medium heat, heat oil.
4. Stir in onions; increase heat to medium-high.
5. Cook, stirring frequently, until onions are tender, about 6 minutes.
6. Add garlic to soup pot, stir; cook 1 minute.
7. Add chicken broth; stir well, scraping bottom of pot to remove any brown bits.
8. Add 1 cup to the mashed potatoes; stir to warm them.
9. Add mashed potatoes to broth.
10. Add corn, bay leaf, thyme, and salt and pepper to taste.

11. Cover pot; increase heat to high and bring soup back to a boil.
12. When soup boils, remove pot from heat and turn off stove.
13. Remove bay leaves.
14. Stir in sour cream until all is well blended.
15. When ready to serve, ladle into individual soup bowls.
16. Sprinkle coarsely chopped bacon over the top.

Yields: 5 servings.

Kremithosoupa (Onion Soup)

This is a simple, hearty onion soup with a tomato base that is great for lunch or as an entrée to dinner.

Ingredients:

2 c. onions, peeled, chopped
½ c. olive oil
2 potatoes, peeled, washed, cubed
2 c. tomato sauce
1 c. water or beef broth
salt and pepper, to taste
parsley leaves, chopped, for garnish

Directions:

1. In large saucepan, place onions and oil; sauté lightly.
2. Add potatoes and tomato sauce, stirring well.
3. Fill with enough water or broth to cover.
4. Add salt and pepper to taste.
5. Boil over medium heat for 30 minutes, until vegetables are tender and flavors blended.
6. Remove from heat and serve with parsley garnish.

French Onion Soup with Dark Beer

The beauty of this soup is that it can be prepared ahead of time, refrigerated, and kept for a few days, while still keeping its freshness and delicious taste.

Ingredients:

½ c. butter
2 lb. onions, peeled, sliced thin
1½ tsp. paprika
6 c. beef stock
½ c. olive oil
½ c. flour
¾ tsp. celery salt
8 oz. dark beer
12 slices French bread, cut into cubes
12 slices Swiss Gruyere cheese
Parmesan cheese

Directions:

1. In medium pot, over medium-high heat, cook onions with butter, stirring often, until onions are brown but not burned, for 30 minutes.
2. Add paprika, and beef stock; bring to boil.
3. In a saucepan, over medium heat, make a roux by whisking the oil and flour together, stirring constantly to avoid burning, until a rich brown.
4. Stir roux into the soup.
5. Add celery salt and simmer at least 2 hours.
6. Remove from heat to add the beer.
7. Cool to a serving temperature; cover and hold until ready to serve.
8. Place cubed bread on baking sheet.
9. Sprinkle with Parmesan cheese and place in a 400 degrees F. oven to toast lightly.

10. Ladle the soup into individual bowls, top with the toasted cheese bread.
11. Place a slice of Gruyere cheese over the top of each bowl; place under broiler just until cheese is melted, bubbly and slightly browned.
12. Remove from oven and serve immediately.

Rich Onion Soup

This is an especially delicious variation of the ever-popular onion soup.

Ingredients:

2 Tbs. butter, softened
3 Tbs. flour
1 c. onion, sliced thinly
1 Tbs. canola oil
3 c. chicken broth
½ c. heavy cream
1 Tbs. fresh basil leaves, ;lightly chopped
salt and pepper, to taste
croutons, for garnish

Directions:

1. In small bowl, knead butter and flour together with your hands.
2. In saucepan, sauté onion in oil over moderate heat, stirring until softened.
3. Add broth and bring to boil.
4. Whisk in butter mixture in small batches, blending until soup thickens.
5. Stir in cream, basil, and salt and pepper to taste.
6. Bring soup just to a boil.
7. Remove from heat and cover until ready to serve.
8. When ready to serve, ladle into individual bowls and sprinkle croutons over soup if desired.

Irish Onion Soup

This is an easy-to-make Irish Soup with the wonderful flavor of onions blended with potatoes and chicken broth. This is a very hearty soup, great on a cold winter's day.

Ingredients:

2 Tbs. butter
1 c. green onions, chopped
3 med. potatoes, peeled, diced
6 c. chicken broth or prepared bouillon
½ lb. Chinese pea pods
¾ c. plain yogurt
1 can sliced water chestnuts, drained (8 oz.)
½ tsp. salt
⅛ tsp. pepper
¼ tsp. ground ginger
⅛ tsp. dry mustard
green onions, sliced

Directions:

1. In 2-quart saucepan, melt butter.
2. Add chopped green onions; sauté until soft.
3. Add potatoes and broth; cover and simmer 20 minutes, or until potatoes are tender.
4. Remove from heat, cool.
5. Purée half of the mixture in blender; return to pan.
6. Remove stems from pea pods; cut each pod, at an angle, into several pieces and set aside.
7. Stir 2 tablespoons purée into the yogurt, and then add the yogurt back to the remaining potatoes.
8. Stir in pea pods, water chestnuts, salt, pepper, ginger, and dry mustard.
9. Over medium heat, bring to a boil.
10. Cover and remove from heat.
11. When ready to serve, pour into individual bowls.
12. Garnish with sliced green onions.
13. Serve immediately.

Potato and Onion Soup

Leeks add unique flavor to this hearty onion and potato soup.

Ingredients:

⅔ c. butter, divided
1 onion, thinly sliced
3 leeks, cleaned, sliced
4 red potatoes, peeled if desired, sliced
2 qt. water
1 Tbs. salt
½ c. heavy whipping cream
3 Tbs. fresh chives, chopped
fresh chives, chopped, for garnish

Directions:

1. In heavy 4-quart saucepan, melt ⅓ cup of butter and sauté onion until wilted.
2. Add leeks, potatoes, water, and salt; bring to boil.
3. Reduce heat and simmer, partially covered, for 45 minutes, or until potatoes are very tender.
4. Remove from heat and cool.
5. Blend cooked mixture until smooth.
6. Return to saucepan
7. Add remainder of butter, cream, and chives.
8. Add more seasoning if needed.
9. Heat again, but do not boil.
10. To serve, ladle into serving bowls.
11. Garnish with additional chopped chives on the top if desired.

Did You Know? . . . .

Did you know that in Spades, Indiana, no onions can be purchased after 6 P.M. without a doctor's prescription?

Root Vegetable Soup

This is an inexpensive and rich soup that may easily be made vegetarian by substituting the chicken stock with vegetable stock.

Ingredients:

2 lb. sweet potatoes, peeled, cut in half lengthwise
2 Tbs. olive oil
1 Tbs. butter
2 lb. carrots, peeled, sliced
2 leeks, white part, sliced (reserve green stem)
6 garlic cloves, peeled, chopped
4 c. chicken stock
2 c. heavy cream
2 Tbs. sugar
salt and pepper, to taste
leek green stem, chopped, for garnish

Directions:

1. Preheat oven to 350 degrees F.
2. Parboil sweet potatoes; slice and place on baking sheet.
3. Roast for 30 minutes, or until lightly browned.
4. In large, heavy saucepan, over medium heat, heat oil and butter.
5. Add carrots, leeks, garlic, and sweet potatoes.
6. Sauté until leeks are translucent, 8 minutes.
7. Add stock and cream.
8. Cover and simmer, stirring occasionally, for 30 minutes, until carrots and potatoes are very soft.
9. Using potato masher, mash vegetables in soup until well mashed.
10. Add salt, pepper, and sugar. Taste and adjust seasonings.

11. When ready to serve, ladle into individual serving bowls.
12. Garnish with a sprinkle of chopped green leek stem.

Smoky Bacon, Potato, and Onion Soup

This is a delicious, hearty soup that is sure to satisfy. Serve with a tossed salad and hot, crusty dinner rolls to complete your meal.

Ingredients:

- 2 Tbs. butter
- 2 Tbs. canola oil
- ¾ c. smoked bacon, finely chopped
- 1¼ c. onions, finely chopped
- 2½ c. potatoes, peeled, finely chopped
- 2 c. chicken stock or broth
- 2 c. milk
- 1 Tbs. fresh parsley, chopped
- salt and pepper, to taste

Directions:

1. In large saucepan, melt butter and oil.
2. Add chopped bacon and cook for a few minutes.
3. Cover and sweat on simmer until soft but not colored.
4. Add stock and potatoes; continue to cook and stir until it becomes quite thick and sticky.
5. Season with salt and pepper.
6. Continue stirring while adding the milk slowly.
7. Cook until the potato disintegrates into a purée.
8. Add parsley.
9. Add additional chicken stock or milk if the soup is too thick.
10. Cover and keep warm until ready to serve.

Three Onion Soup

Leeks and green onions combine to give delicious flavor to this onion soup.

Ingredients:

4 Tbs. olive oil
3 lg. sweet onions, your choice, thinly sliced
8 green onions, thinly sliced
4 leeks, white part only, thinly sliced
6 garlic cloves, chopped
2 Tbs. flour
8 c. beef or chicken broth, or combination
½ tsp. ground nutmeg
1 c. red wine
8 slices French bread
6 oz. Swiss cheese, grated, divided

Directions:

1. Place oil in Dutch oven and heat.
2. Add onions, green onions, leeks, and garlic; sauté until translucent.
3. Mix in flour to make a roux (a mixture of flour and fat cooked together and used for thickening).
4. Sauté until mixture just starts to turn golden.
5. Add broth, wine, and nutmeg.
6. At this point, taste broth for flavor and seasoning.
7. If broth does not meet expectations, add a chicken or beef bouillon cube, or ½ teaspoon of chicken or beef base.
8. Taste broth again and make adjustments until you are satisfied with the flavor.
9. Stir and simmer on low heat for 25 minutes.
10. Spoon into bowls that can be placed under the broiler.
11. Top with French bread and cheese.
12. Place bowls under broiler.
13. Broil until cheese melts and is bubbly.

Tuscan Onion Soup

If you enjoy the flavor of Italian bacon or pancetta, you will enjoy this soup.

Ingredients:

½ c. pancetta, diced
1 Tbs. olive oil
4 lg. white onions, thinly sliced
3 garlic cloves, minced
3¾ c. reduced sodium chicken broth
1 tsp. dried parsley flakes
4 slices Italian bread
3 Tbs. butter, soft
¾ c. Swiss cheese, coarsely grated
salt and freshly ground pepper, to taste

Directions:

1. In large saucepan, over medium heat, sauté pancetta until it starts to brown; remove and set aside.
2. Add oil and onions.
3. Cook on high heat for 4 minutes.
4. Stir in garlic; reduce heat to low.
5. Cover and cook until onions are a soft golden brown.
6. Add chicken broth, parsley, salt, and pepper.
7. Bring to boil; reduce heat and simmer uncovered for 15 minutes.
8. While soup is cooking, heat broiler and toast bread on both sides.
9. Butter one side of toast; sprinkle with cheese, and cut into bite-size pieces.
10. When ready to serve the soup, stir in the reserved pancetta.
11. Serve topped with toasted cheese croutons.

Six Onion Soup

Do try this interesting onion soup recipe. It contains six different types of onions, giving you an opportunity to discover your favorites.

Ingredients:

- 5 Tbs. sweet butter
- 1 c. yellow onion, finely chopped
- ⅔ c. sweet onion, finely chopped
- ⅔ c. red onion, finely chopped
- 5 lg. leeks, white part, cleaned, thinly sliced
- ⅔ c. shallots, chopped
- 5 garlic cloves, peeled, minced
- 4 c. chicken or vegetable stock
- 1 tsp. dried thyme
- 1 bay leaf
- 1½ c. heavy cream
- 4 scallions, cleaned, diagonally cut into ½-inch pieces
- salt and freshly ground black pepper, to taste
- toasted French bread croutons, for garnish
- fresh chives, snipped, for garnish

Directions:

1. In large pot, melt butter.
2. Add onions, leeks, shallots, and garlic.
3. Over low heat, cook, covered, 25 minutes, until vegetables are tender and lightly colored.
4. Add stock, thyme, and bay leaf.
5. Season to taste with salt and pepper.
6. Bring to boil; reduce heat and cook, partially covered, for 20 minutes.
7. Pour soup through strainer placed over bowl.
8. Transfer solids and 1 cup of the liquid to a blender; purée.
9. Return purée and remaining 3 cups liquid to pot and set over medium heat.
10. Whisk in heavy cream and bring to a simmer.
11. Add scallions and simmer for another 5 minutes, or until tender.
12. Ladle into heated bowls.
13. Garnish with croutons of toasted French bread.
14. Sprinkle the snipped fresh chives over the top.

Vegetarian Onion Soup

My two vegetarian daughters look forward to this soup. Actually, the entire family enjoys this vegetarian version with lots of Gouda cheese.

Ingredients:

½ c. butter
1 tsp. white pepper, freshly ground
5 c. yellow onions, thinly sliced
1½ c. dry white wine
4 c. water
¼ c. parsley, chopped, packed
2 Tbs. dark soy sauce
1 tsp. dried thyme
2 bay leaves
2 whole cloves
4 thick slices French bread, toasted
5 c. Gouda cheese, grated

Directions:

1. In large saucepan, over medium heat, melt butter.
2. Add onions and pepper, stirring to coat onions.
3. Continue to cook for 30 minutes, stirring often.
4. Add wine and stir 3 minutes, deglazing pot.
5. Bring to boil.
6. Add water, parsley, soy sauce, thyme, bay leaves, and cloves.
7. Return to boiling; reduce heat to a simmer and cook another 30 minutes.
8. Remove from heat; cover, and let stand for 1 hour.
9. Discard bay leaves and cloves.
10. Ladle soup into ovenproof bowls or ramekins.
11. Place 1 toast slice on top of each serving and divide cheese evenly on top of toast.
12. Place under broiler and allow cheese to melt and bubble; be careful not to burn or overcook!
13. Serve while hot.

White Onion Soup

This recipe is an interesting variation of onion soup, using white onions and white wine. It is further set off by the flavor of blue cheese. Enjoy!

Ingredients for croutons:

1 French baguette
4 Tbs. butter, softened
4 Tbs. blue cheese

Ingredients for soup:

¼ c. olive oil
2 lb. white onions, peeled, thinly sliced
8 c. chicken broth or vegetable broth
¾ c. flour
¾ c. white wine
2 bay leaves
salt and pepper, to taste

Directions for croutons:

1. Preheat oven to 375 degrees F.
2. Cut baguette into thin slices.
3. Butter both sides.
4. Arrange in single layer on baking sheet.
5. Bake 8 to 10 minutes, until lightly toasted.
6. Sprinkle with cheese.
7. Return to oven for a few minutes, just until cheese melts.
8. Remove from oven and set aside for soup topping.

Directions for soup:

1. In Dutch oven, over medium-high heat, heat oil until it just begins to faintly smoke.
2. Add onions and sauté 2 minutes; stir occasionally.
3. Reduce heat, cover and cook 5 more minutes, stirring occasionally.

4. In small saucepan, over medium heat, bring broth to simmer; reserve.
5. Stir flour into onions and add wine.
6. Gradually stir reserved hot broth into onions.
7. Add bay leaves; add salt and pepper, to taste.
8. Simmer 10 to 15 minutes.
9. Remove and discard bay leaves.
10. Ladle into warmed soup bowls.
11. Top each serving with blue cheese croutons.

Broccoli Onion Soup

Try this delicious broccoli and onion soup with your favorite bread or crackers.

Ingredients:

1 med. sweet onion, chopped
2 Tbs. butter
2 pkg. cream cheese, cubed (8 oz. each)
2 c. milk
2 chicken bouillon cubes
1½ c. boiling water
1 pkg. broccoli, chopped, cooked, drained (10 oz.)
1 tsp. lemon juice
1 tsp. salt
¼ tsp. pepper

Directions:

1. In skillet, over low heat, sauté onion in butter until tender.
2. Add cream cheese and milk; stir until cheese is melted.
3. Dissolve bouillon in boiling water.
4. Add to cream cheese mixture.
5. Stir in broccoli, lemon juice, salt, and pepper.
6. Heat thoroughly.

Yields: 6 servings.

Onion Soup Atu

This is another great onion soup. It is delicious with the French baguette and all the cheeses.

Ingredients:

1 French baguette
3 Tbs. butter
2 onions, thinly sliced
¼ c. flour
2 cans beef consommé
5 c. water, hot
¼ tsp. salt
¼ tsp. ground black pepper
¼ tsp. garlic powder
4 Tbs. ketchup
2 Tbs. hot sauce
1 beef bouillon cube
¾ c. sharp Cheddar cheese, shredded
¾ c. Swiss cheese, shredded
¾ c. Parmesan cheese, grated
8 slices Gruyere cheese

Directions:

1. Preheat oven to 325 degrees F.
2. Cut French baguette into ¾-inch slices.
3. Place directly on rack in oven for 20 minutes, or until bread is dry and lightly browned; remove and set aside.
4. In heavy bottomed saucepan, melt butter.
5. Add onions, and sauté over low heat for 15 minutes, or until lightly browned.
6. Sprinkle onions with flour.
7. Stir while cooking for 2 minutes, or until flour is well blended.
8. Add beef consommé, water, salt, pepper, garlic powder, ketchup, hot sauce, and beef bouillon cube.
9. Bring to boil; simmer 20 minutes.
10. Combine cheeses in a mixing bowl.
11. Set oven temperature to broil.

12. Ladle soup into ovenproof soup bowls.
13. Top each bowl with a slice of toasted French baguette bread.
14. Sprinkle mixed cheese over bread and place one slice of Gruyere cheese on top.
15. Place soup bowls under broiler.
16. Broil until cheese is melted, bubbly, and lightly browned, about 2 to 3 minutes.
17. Serve immediately with remaining baguette bread slices on the side.

Onion Soup

This is an easy-to-make onion soup. Serve with your favorite crackers or bread.

Ingredients:

4 Tbs. butter
1 lg. Spanish onion, thinly sliced
2 Tbs. flour
2 cans beef consommé (10 oz.)
1 c. water or dry white wine
2 Tbs. Parmesan cheese
salt and pepper, to taste

Directions:

1. In skillet, over low heat, melt butter.
2. Increase heat to medium. Brown onion slices 5 to 6 minutes, stirring frequently using a wooden spoon.
3. Sprinkle flour over onion slices; stir until well mixed.
4. Slowly pour in consommé; add water or wine.
5. Increase heat to high; bring to a boil.
6. Reduce heat to medium; cover skillet and cook for 7 to 10 minutes, stirring occasionally.
7. Remove from heat; season with salt and pepper to taste.
8. Stir in cheese until melted.
9. Pour onion soup into individual bowls and serve.

Japanese Onion Soup

Try this version of onion soup. It is very mild, a bit salty, and slightly tangy. Use your favorite mushrooms in this recipe.

Ingredients:

½ stalk celery, chopped
1 sm. onion, chopped
½ carrot, chopped
1 tsp. fresh gingerroot, grated
¼ tsp. fresh garlic, minced
2 Tbs. chicken stock
3 tsp. beef bouillon granules
1 c. fresh shiitake mushrooms, chopped
2 qt. water
1 c. baby portobello mushrooms, sliced
1 Tbs. fresh chives, minced

Directions:

1. In a large saucepan or stockpot, combine celery, onion, carrot, ginger, garlic, and a few mushrooms.
2. Add chicken stock, beef bouillon, and water.
3. Over high heat, bring to a rolling boil.
4. Cover; reduce heat to medium, and cook for 45 minutes.
5. Place remaining mushrooms into a large pot.
6. When soup is done, place a strainer over the pot with the mushrooms in it.
7. Strain the cooked soup into the pot with the mushrooms. Discard strained materials.
8. Serve the broth with mushrooms in small soup bowls.
9. Sprinkle fresh chives over the top.

Yields: 6 servings.

Onion Delights Cookbook

A Collection of Onion Recipes
Cookbook Delights Series-Book 8

Wines and Spirits

Table of Contents

Page

About Cooking with Alcohol

Some recipes in this cookbook contain, among other ingredients, liquors. It is for the purpose of obtaining desired flavor and achieving culinary appreciation and not to be abused in any way. In cooking and baking, alcohol evaporates and only the flavor may be enjoyed. When mixed in cold, however, such as in desserts, caution must be exercised. These recipes are intended for people who may consume small amounts of alcohol in a responsible and safe manner.

I live in Washington State and we are proud of our wine production. Washington State is rapidly gaining prestige as a premier wine producer. Do enjoy the art of wine tasting and enjoy the completeness and uniqueness of each wine. It is an art to enjoy and savor in moderation.

If consumption of even small amounts of alcoholic ingredients presents a problem, in whatever form, please substitute coffee flavor syrups, found in coffee sections of supermarkets. For example, instead of Southern Comfort liqueur, substitute with Irish Cream or Amaretto Syrup.

Karen Jean Matsko Hood

Bloody Bull

This is a delicious drink with just the right blend of flavors.

Ingredients:

1 oz. vodka
½ glass tomato juice
½ glass beef bouillon
1 tsp. onion powder
1 lime slice
1 lemon wedge

Directions:

1. Place vodka, tomato juice, onion powder, and beef bouillon into a shaker jar; shake well.
2. Pour over ice in a highball glass and stir.
3. To serve, add the slice of lime and the wedge of lemon.

Gent of the Jury

This is a simple yet tasty drink.

Ingredients:

2 oz. gin
1½ tsp. dry vermouth
3 cocktail onions

Directions:

1. In mixing glass half-filled with ice cubes, combine gin and vermouth; stir well.
2. Strain into chilled cocktail glass.
3. Garnish with onions.

Haiku Martini

Japanese sake adds an interesting taste to this martini.

Ingredients:

2 oz. sake
1 dash dry Vermouth
1 cocktail onion

Directions:

1. In a mixing glass half filled with ice cubes, combine the sake and vermouth; stir well.
2. Strain into chilled cocktail glass.
3. Garnish with a cocktail onion.

Patton Martini

This martini uses both onions and olives, for a decidedly Mediterranean taste.

Ingredients:

1½ oz. gin
1 splash dry vermouth
1 dash olive juice
2 cocktail onions
2 olives

Directions:

1. Mix gin, vermouth, and olive juice in cocktail shaker with ice.
2. Shake; immediately strain into chilled cocktail glass.
3. Garnish with onions and olives alternately on a toothpick.

Bloody Mary Party Drink

This can be served at parties and other evening get-togethers. It is unusual with the cooked vegetables, but it is full of flavor.

Ingredients:

2½ c. onions, minced
2 c. celery, minced
1¼ c. cucumber, peeled, seeded, minced
8 lg. garlic cloves, minced
2 Tbs. butter
4 cans tomato juice (46 oz. ea.)
1½ c. lemon juice
3 Tbs. sugar
½ tsp. red pepper sauce
½ tsp. Worcestershire sauce
1 bottle of vodka (a fifth)
½ c. green onions, sliced

Directions:

1. In skillet, melt butter.
2. Sauté onion, celery, cucumber, and garlic until soft.
3. Add tomato juice, lemon juice, sugar, red pepper sauce, and Worcestershire sauce.
4. Simmer 7 to 8 minutes.
5. Remove from heat; cool and then chill.
6. Place vodka bottle in a can filled with water.
7. Freeze until ice is solid.
8. Remove can.
9. Keep vodka surrounded in ice and wrapped in a towel.
10. Portion drink into serving cups.
11. Add 1 oz. jigger of vodka per serving.
12. Garnish with a sprinkle of green onion.

Bloody Mary Surprise

Try this delicious, spicy drink that is made with homemade tomato juice. Enjoy!

Ingredients:

6 lb. fresh tomatoes (32 oz.)
4 Tbs. red onion, finely chopped
1 jalapeno pepper, finely chopped
4 Tbs. cucumber, finely chopped
2 Tbs. hot sauce
6 jiggers Vodka
4 celery stalks, for garnish
1 lime, cut into quarters for garnish
4 jumbo shrimp, cooked, for garnish
juice of 2 limes
salt, to taste
fresh ground pepper, to taste
hot sauce, to taste

Directions:

1. To prepare the tomato juice: Begin with very ripe, juicy tomatoes. The better the flavor of the tomatoes, the better the juice. For every quart of juice, you will need 2 quarts of fresh tomatoes.
2. Chop the tomatoes coarsely.
3. Place tomatoes in a stainless steel pot.
4. Over low heat, bring to a simmer.
5. Cook until the tomatoes soften completely and their juices are released.
6. Remove from heat; cool.
7. Run the tomatoes and juice through a food mill, fine sieve, or juicer to remove the seeds and skin.
8. Pour the tomato purée into a bowl and let stand for 30 minutes. Tomatoes that contain a significant amount of water may separate, causing the water to

rise to the top. If this happens, skim off the water. If necessary, keep skimming as long as the juice keeps separating. The more water you remove, the thicker the tomato juice.

9. Taste the juice. Remember, this is not canned. It might taste slightly bland without the salt, sugar, and citric acid used by commercial canners to bring out the flavors. It should have a heavy, rich tomato aroma, and if the flavor doesn't quite meet your specifications, add salt, sugar or lemon juice to suit your palate. Refrigerate the juice immediately. It will keep for a few days, but the flavor diminishes with time.
10. In a 2-quart pitcher, combine the tomato juice with everything except the celery and lime wedges.
11. Pour into 4 tall glasses full of ice.
12. Garnish with a celery stalk and lime wedge on each.
13. If you are in a flamboyant mood, top each Bloody Mary with a cooked, chilled jumbo prawn.
14. Note: In the absence of fresh tomatoes, we use either V-8 juice or canned tomato juice, and the results are still spectacular!

Kooch

You will love this drink if you like the taste of peppermint.

Ingredients:

1 oz. peppermint schnapps
1 oz. clam juice

Directions:

1. In shaker jar, combine both ingredients.
2. Pour into a highball glass with ice.
3. Garnish with a cocktail onion.

Spring Onion Cocktail

Enjoy this delicious spring onion cocktail.

Ingredients:

- 7 fresh Italian parsley sprigs
- 3 Tbs. gin
- 8 very thin slices green onion tops
- 1½ Tbs. fresh lemon juice
- 1 Tbs. white grape juice
- 1 Tbs. simple syrup
- 2 tsp. pickling liquid (pickled pearl onion liquid)
- 1 c. ice cubes
- 5 pickled pearl onions

Directions:

1. Using handle of wooden spoon, mash parsley in cocktail shaker.
2. Add gin and next 6 ingredients.
3. Cover; shake vigorously.
4. Pour or strain contents, including ice, into tall glass.
5. Mix in pearl onions.

Grenadine Martini

Try this version of a martini with a splash of Grenadine. Enjoy!

Ingredients:

- 1 oz. gin
- 1 oz. scotch
- 3 oz. lime juice
- splash of Grenadine

Directions:

1. Combine first 3 ingredients in a shaker jar.
2. Add a splash of Grenadine.
3. Shake well.
4. Place crushed ice into a chilled martini glass.
5. Garnish with a cocktail onion.

Brandy Cocktail

This is a delicious cocktail. Enjoy!

Ingredients:

3 parts cognac
1 part vermouth, sweet
2 dashes Bitters
cocktail onion
lemon

Directions:

1. Chill a cocktail glass in the freezer.
2. Pour cognac and vermouth into a mixing glass.
3. Fill the mixing glass with ice cubes and stir.
4. Strain the drink into the cocktail glass.
5. Garnish with a cocktail onion and a lemon peel.

Did You Know? . . . .

Did you know that in Nacogdoches, Texas, if you would like to take your date for a delicious hamburger and onions, that there is a strict onion curfew for "young women?" Under no circumstances are they allowed to have any raw onions after 6 P.M.

Yellow Rattler

The orange juice adds a refreshing flavor to the gin and vermouth.

Ingredients:

1 oz. gin
½ oz. sweet vermouth
½ oz. dry vermouth
1 Tbs. orange juice
1 cocktail onion

Directions:

1. Shake together both vermouths and orange juice with ice.
2. Strain into chilled cocktail glass.
3. Add cocktail onion and serve.

Gibson Martini

Martinis are not only excellent, but also sophisticated.

Ingredients:

6 parts gin or vodka
1 part dry vermouth
3 cocktail onions

Directions:

1. Shake or stir gin (or vodka) and vermouth with ice.
2. Strain into a chilled martini glass.
3. Spear onions with a toothpick or cocktail pick.
4. Place in glass for garnish.

Pearl of Wisdom

Try this delicious drink at your next get-together. Join in the fun!

Ingredients:

1 oz. dry white sake
1 oz. cherry brandy
1 oz. gin
2 oz. sweet and sour mix
juice from ½ a lime
splash of club soda
pearl onion

Directions:

1. Place a pearl onion "the pearl" in the bottom of a tall glass.
2. Cover with 2 inches of crushed ice.
3. In shaker jar, add all ingredients except club soda.
4. Shake well.
5. Strain into the prepared glass.
6. Add club soda.
7. Garnish with a lime wheel and a pair of chopsticks.
8. Place a fortune cookie on the rim of the glass.
9. Once served, the idea is to retrieve the "pearl" with the chop sticks then learn your fortune from the cookie.

Did You Know? . . . .

Did you know a woman has the legal right to make her wayward spouse eat raw onions when she catches him drinking? The law in Wolf Point, Montana, says such action is her "moral, wifely duty."

Blue Curacao Splash

If you are looking for a splash of blue, this is the perfect drink.

Ingredients:

- 1 sugar cube
- 1 splash angostura bitters
- ⅓ c. champagne or sparkling wine
- 4 tsp. vodka
- 2 tsp. blue Curacao
- 1 cocktail onion

Directions:

1. Splash a puddle of angostura bitters into saucer and place sugar cube in it to soak, 1 to 2 minutes.
2. Stir champagne, vodka, and blue Curacao together in a container.
3. Chill in refrigerator.
4. When ready to serve, place soaked sugar cube in the bottom of champagne glass.
5. Pour in alcohol mixture.
6. Drop in cocktail onion, which should float loose, not on a cocktail stick.
7. Serve.

Did You Know? . . . .

Did you know that onions can not be eaten in Budds Creek, Maryland, except by people over 21 who have written permission from their dentist?

Did you know that there is a loony law in Wilmington, Delaware, that makes it illegal for anyone to slurp their onion soup in a restaurant?

Festival Information

Vidalia Onion Festival
The last weekend in April every year
Vidalia, GA
General Information: For general festival info and air show tickets, call the Vidalia Area Convention and Visitors Bureau at (912) 538-8687, (912) 608-4013 or email vacvb@bellsouth.net

Walla Walla Sweet Onion Festival
Mid-July
County Fairgrounds, Walla Walla, Washington

Onion Associations and Commissions

Idaho Onion Growers Association
P.O. Box 430
Parma, ID 83660
Phone: (208) 722-5044
Fax: (208) 722-7330

National Onion Association
822 7th Street Suite 510
Greeley, CO 80631
Phone: (970) 353-5895
Fax: (970) 353-5897

Vidalia Onion Committee
P.O. Box 1609
Vidalia, GA 30475
Phone: (912) 537-1918
Fax: (912) 537-2166

U.S. and Metric Measurement Charts

Here are some measurement equivalents to help you with exchanges. There was a time when many people thought the entire world would convert to the metric scale. While most of the world has, America still has not. Metric conversions in cooking are vitally important to preparing a tasty recipe. Here are simple conversion tables that should come in handy.

U.S. Measurement Equivalents

a few grains/pinch/dash (dry) = less than ⅛ teaspoon
a dash (liquid) = a few drops
3 teaspoons = 1 tablespoon
½ tablespoon = 1½ teaspoons
1 tablespoon = 3 teaspoons
2 tablespoons = 1 fluid ounce
4 tablespoons = ¼ cup
5⅓ tablespoons = ⅓ cup
8 tablespoons = ½ cup
8 tablespoons = 4 fluid ounces
10⅔ tablespoons = ⅔ cup
12 tablespoons = ¾ cup
16 tablespoons = 1 cup
16 tablespoons = 8 fluid ounces
⅛ cup = 2 tablespoons
¼ cup = 4 tablespoons
¼ cup = 2 fluid ounces
⅓ cup = 5 tablespoons plus 1 teaspoon
½ cup = 8 tablespoons
1 cup = 16 tablespoons
1 cup = 8 fluid ounces
1 cup = ½ pint
2 cups = 1 pint
2 pints = 1 quart
4 quarts (liquid) = 1 gallon
8 quarts (dry) = 1 peck
4 pecks (dry) = 1 bushel
1 kilogram = approximately 2 pounds
1 liter=approximately 4 cups or 1quart

Approximate Metric Equivalents by Volume

U.S.	Metric
¼ cup = 60 milliliters	
½ cup = 120 milliliters	
1 cup = 230 milliliters	
1¼ cups = 300 milliliters	
1½ cups = 360 milliliters	
2 cups = 460 milliliters	
2½ cups = 600 milliliters	
3 cups = 700 milliliters	
4 cups (1 quart) = .95 liter	
1.06 quarts = 1 liter	
4 quarts (1 gallon) = 3.8 liters	

Approximate Metric Equivalents by Weight

U.S.	Metric
¼ ounce = 7 grams	
½ ounce = 14 grams	
1 ounce = 28 grams	
1¼ ounces = 35 grams	
1½ ounces = 40 grams	
2½ ounces = 70 grams	
4 ounces = 112 grams	
5 ounces = 140 grams	
8 ounces = 228 grams	
10 ounces = 280 grams	
15 ounces = 425 grams	
16 ounces (1 pound) = 454 grams	

Glossary

Aerate: A synonym for sift; to pass ingredients through a fine-mesh device to break up large pieces and incorporate air into ingredients to make them lighter.

Al dente: "To the tooth," in Italian. The pasta is cooked just enough to maintain a firm, chewy texture.

Baste: To brush or spoon liquid fat or juices over meat during roasting to add flavor and prevent drying out.

Bias-slice**:** To slice a food crosswise at a 45-degree angle.

Bind: To thicken a sauce or hot liquid by stirring in ingredients such as eggs, flour, butter, or cream until it holds together.

Blackened: Popular Cajun-style cooking method. Seasoned foods are cooked over high heat in a super-heated heavy skillet until charred.

Blanch: To scald, as in vegetables being prepared for freezing; as in almonds so as to remove skins.

Blend: To mix or fold two or more ingredients together to obtain equal distribution throughout the mixture.

Braise: To brown meat in oil or other fat and then cook slowly in liquid. The effect of braising is to tenderize the meat.

Bread: To coat food with crumbs (usually with soft or dry bread crumbs), sometimes seasoned.

Brown: To quickly sauté, broil, or grill either at the beginning or at the end of meal preparation, often to enhance flavor, texture, or eye appeal.

Brush: To use a pastry brush to coat a food such as meat or pastry with melted butter, glaze, or other liquid.

Butterfly: To cut open a food such as pork chops down the center without cutting all the way through, and then spread apart.

Caramelization: Browning sugar over a flame, with or without the addition of some water to aid the process. The temperature range in which sugar caramelizes is approximately 320 to 360 degrees F.

Clarify: To remove impurities from butter or stock by heating the liquid, then straining or skimming it.

Coddle: A cooking method in which foods (such as eggs) are put in separate containers and placed in a pan of simmering water for slow, gentle cooking.

Confit: To slowly cook pieces of meat in their own gently rendered fat.

Core: To remove the inedible center of fruits such as pineapples.

Cream: To beat vegetable shortening, butter, or margarine, with or without sugar, until light and fluffy. This process traps in air bubbles, later used to create height in cookies and cakes.

Crimp: To create a decorative edge on a pie crust. On a double pie crust, this also seals the edges together.

Curd: A custard-like pie or tart filling flavored with juice and zest of citrus fruit, usually lemon, although lime and orange may also be used.

Curdle: To cause semisolid pieces of coagulated protein to develop in food, usually as a result of the addition of an acid substance, or the overheating of milk or egg-based sauces.

Custard: A mixture of beaten egg, milk, and possibly other ingredients such as sweet or savory flavorings, which are cooked with gentle heat, often in a water bath or double boiler. As pie filling, the custard is frequently cooked and chilled before being layered into a baked crust.

Deglaze: To add liquid to a pan in which foods have been fried or roasted, in order to dissolve the caramelized juices stuck to the bottom of the pan.

Dot: To sprinkle food with small bits of an ingredient such as butter to allow for even melting.

Dredge: To sprinkle lightly and evenly with sugar or flour. A dredger has holes pierced on the lid to sprinkle evenly.

Drippings: The liquids left in the bottom of a roasting or frying pan after meat is cooked. Drippings are generally used for gravies and sauces.

Drizzle: To pour a liquid such as a sweet glaze or melted butter in a slow, light trickle over food.

Dust: To sprinkle food lightly with spices, sugar, or flour for a light coating.

Egg Wash: A mixture of beaten eggs (yolks, whites, or whole eggs) with either milk or water. Used to coat cookies and other baked goods to give them a shine when baked.

Emulsion: A mixture of liquids, one being a fat or oil and the other being water based so that tiny globules of one are suspended in the other. This may involve the use of stabilizers, such as egg or custard. Emulsions may be temporary or permanent.

Entrée: A French term that originally referred to the first course of a meal, served after the soup and before the meat courses. In the United States, it refers to the main dish of a meal.

Fillet: To remove the bones from meat or fish for cooking.

Filter: To remove lumps, excess liquid, or impurities by passing through paper or cheesecloth.

Firm-Ball Stage**:** In candy making, the point at which boiling syrup dropped in cold water forms a ball that is compact yet gives slightly to the touch.

Flambé: To ignite a sauce or other liquid so that it flames.

Flan: An open pie filled with sweet or savory ingredients; also, a Spanish dessert of baked custard covered with caramel.

Flute: To create a decorative scalloped or undulating edge on a pie crust or other pastry.

Fricassee: Usually a stew in which the meat is cut up, lightly cooked in butter, and then simmered in liquid until done.

Frizzle: To cook thin slices of meat in hot oil until crisp and slightly curly.

Ganache: A rich chocolate filling or coating made with chocolate, vegetable shortening, and possibly heavy cream. It can coat cakes or cookies, and be used as a filling for truffles.

Glaze: A liquid that gives an item a shiny surface. Examples are fruit jams that have been heated or chocolate thinned with melted vegetable shortening. Also, to cover a food with such a liquid.

Gratin: To bind together or combine food with a liquid such as cream, milk, béchamel sauce, or tomato sauce, in a shallow dish. The mixture is then baked until cooked and set.

Hard-Ball Stage**:** In candy making, the point at which syrup has cooked long enough to form a solid ball in cold water.

Hull (also husk): To remove the leafy parts of soft fruits, such as strawberries or blackberries.

Infusion: To extract flavors by soaking them in liquid heated in a covered pan. The term also refers to the liquid resulting from this process.

Jerk or Jamaican Jerk Seasoning: A dry mixture of various spices such as chilies, thyme, garlic, onions, and cinnamon or cloves used to season meats such as chicken or pork.

Julienne: To cut into long, thin strips.

Jus: The natural juices released by roasting meats.

Larding: To inset strips of fat into pieces of meat, so that the braised meat stays moist and juicy.

Marble: To gently swirl one food into another.

Marinate: To combine food with aromatic ingredients to add flavor.

Meringue: Egg whites beaten until they are stiff, then sweetened. It can be used as the topping for pies or baked as cookies.

Mull: To slowly heat cider with spices and sugar.

Parboil: To partly cook in a boiling liquid.

Peaks: The mounds made in a mixture. For example, egg white that has been whipped to stiffness. Peaks are "stiff" if they stay upright or "soft" if they curl over.

Pesto: A sauce usually made of fresh basil, garlic, olive oil, pine nuts, and cheese. The ingredients are finely chopped and then mixed, uncooked, with pasta. Generally, the term refers to any uncooked sauce made of finely chopped herbs and nuts.

Pipe: To force a semisoft food through a bag (either a pastry bag or a plastic bag with one corner cut off) to decorate food.

Pressure Cooking: To cook using steam trapped under a locked lid to produce high temperatures and achieve fast cooking time.

Purée: To mash or sieve food into a thick liquid.

Ramekin: A small baking dish used for individual servings of sweet and savory dishes.

Reduce: To cook liquids down so that some of the water evaporates.

Refresh: To pour cold water over freshly cooked vegetables to prevent further cooking and to retain color.

Roux: A cooked paste usually made from flour and butter used to thicken sauces.

Sauté: To cook foods quickly in a small amount of oil in a skillet or sauté pan over direct heat.

Scald: To heat a liquid, usually a dairy product, until it almost boils.

Sear: To seal in a meat's juices by cooking it quickly using very high heat.

Seize: To form a thick, lumpy mass when melted (usually applies to chocolate).

Sift: To remove large lumps from a dry ingredient such as flour or confectioners' sugar by passing it through a fine mesh. This process also incorporates air into the ingredients, making them lighter.

Simmer: To cook food in a liquid at a low enough temperature that small bubbles begin to break the surface.

Steam: To cook over boiling water in a covered pan. This method keeps foods' shape, texture, and nutritional value intact better than methods such as boiling.

Steep: To soak dry ingredients (tea leaves, ground coffee, herbs, spices, etc.) in liquid until the flavor is infused into the liquid.

Stewing: To brown small pieces of meat, poultry, or fish, then simmer them with vegetables or other ingredients in enough liquid to cover them, usually in a closed pot on the stove, in the oven, or with a slow cooker.

Thin: To reduce a mixture's thickness with the addition of more liquid.

Truss: To use string, skewers, or pins to hold together a food to maintain its shape while it cooks (usually applied to meat or poultry).

Unleavened: Baked goods that contain no agents to give them volume, such as baking powder, baking soda, or yeast.

Vinaigrette: A general term referring to any sauce made with vinegar, oil, and seasonings.

Zest: The thin, brightly colored outer part of the rind of citrus fruits. It contains volatile oils, used as a flavoring.

Recipe Index of Onion Delights

Reader Feedback Form

Dear Reader,

We are very interested in what our readers think. Please fill in the form below and return it to:

Whispering Pine Press International, Inc.
c/o Onion Delights Cookbook
P.O. Box 214, Spokane Valley, WA 99037-0214 USA
Phone: (509) 928-8700 | Fax: (509) 922-9949
Email: sales@WhisperingPinePress.com
Publisher Website: www.WhisperingPinePress.com
Book Website: www.OnionDelightsCookbook.com

Name: ____

Address: ______________________________________

City, St., Zip: _________________________________

Phone/Fax: (____) ______________ / (____) __________

Email: ____

Comments/Suggestions: ___________________________

____

____

____

____

A great deal of care and attention has been exercised in the creation of this book. Designing a great cookbook that is original, fun, and easy to use has been a job that required many hours of diligence, creativity, and research. Although we strive to make this book completely error free, errors and discrepancies may not be completely excluded. If you come across any errors or discrepancies, please make a note of them and send them to our publishing office. We are constantly updating our manuscripts, eliminating errors, and improving quality.

Please contact us at the address above.

About the Cookbook Delights Series

The *Cookbook Delights Series* includes many different topics and themes. If you have a passion for food and wish to know more information about different foods, then this series of cookbooks will be beneficial to you. Each book features a different type of food, such as avocados, strawberries, huckleberries, salmon, vegetarian, lentils, almonds, cherries, coconuts, lemons, and many, many more.

The *Cookbook Delights Series* not only includes cookbooks about individual foods but also includes several holiday-themed cookbooks. Whatever your favorite holiday may be, chances are we have a cookbook with recipes designed with that holiday in mind. Some examples include *Halloween Delights, Thanksgiving Delights, Christmas Delights, Valentine Delights, Mother's Day Delights, St. Patrick's Day Delights,* and *Easter Delights.*

Each cookbook is designed for easy use and is organized into alphabetical sections. Over 250 recipes are included along with other interesting facts, folklore, and history of the featured food or theme. Each book comes with a beautiful full-color cover, ordering information, and a list of other upcoming books in the series.

Note cards, bookmarks, and a daily journal have been printed and are available to go along with each cookbook. You may view the entire line of cookbooks, journals, cards, posters, puzzles, and bookmarks by visiting our website at and www.oniondelights.com, or you can email us with your questions and your comments to: sales@whisperingpinepress.com.

Please ask your local bookstore to carry these sets of books.

To order, please contact:

Whispering Pine Press International, Inc.
c/o Onion Delights Cookbook
P.O. Box 214, Spokane Valley, WA 99037-0214 USA
Phone: (509) 9928-8700| Fax: (509) 922-9949
Email: sales@WhisperingPinePress.com
Publisher Website: www.WhisperingPinePress.com
Book Website: www.OnionDelightsCookbook.com
SAN 253-200X

We Invite You to Join the Whispering Pine Press International, Inc., Book Club!

Whispering Pine Press International, Inc.
c/o Onion Delights Cookbook
P.O. Box 214, Spokane Valley, WA 99037-0214 USA
Phone: (509) 928-8700 l Fax: (509) 922-9949
Email: sales@WhisperingPinePress.com
Publisher Website: www.WhisperingPinePress.com
Book Website: www.OnionDelightsCookbook.com

Buy 11 books and get the next one free, based on the average price of the first eleven purchased.

How the club works:

Simply use the order form below and order books from our catalog. You can buy just one at a time or all eleven at once. After the first eleven books are purchased, the next one is free. Please add shipping and handling as listed on this form. There are no purchase requirements at any time during your membership. Free book credit is based on the average price of the first eleven books purchased.

Join today! Pick your books and mail in the form today!

Yes! I want to join the Whispering Pine Press International, Inc., Book Club! Enroll me and send the books indicated below.

Title Price

1. ______
2. ______
3. ______
4. ______
5. ______
6. ______
7. ______
8. ______
9. ______
10. ______
11. ______

Free Book Title: ______

Free Book Price: ______ Avg. Price: ______ Total Price: ______

Credit for the free book is based on the average price of the first 11 books purchased.

(Circle one) Check | Visa | MasterCard | Discover | American Express

Credit Card #: ______ Expiration Date: ______

Name: ______

Address: ______

City: ______ State: ______ Country: ______

Zip/Postal: ______ Phone: (____) ______

Email: ______

Signature ______

Whispering Pine Press International, Inc.
Fundraising Opportunities

Fundraising cookbooks are proven moneymakers and great keepsake providers for your group. Whispering Pine Press International, Inc., offers a very special personalized cookbook fundraising program that encourages success to organizations all across the USA.

Our prices are competitive and fair. Currently, we offer a special of 100 books with many free features and excellent customer service. Any purchase you make is guaranteed first-rate.

Flexibility is not a problem. If you have special needs, we guarantee our cooperation in meeting each of them. Our goal is to create a cookbook that goes beyond your expectations. We have the confidence and a record that promises continual success.

Another great fundraising program is the *Cookbook Delights Series* Program. With cookbook orders of 50 copies or more, your organization receives a huge discount, making for a prompt and lucrative solution.

We also specialize in assisting group fundraising – Christian, community, nonprofit, and academic among them. If you are struggling for a new idea, something that will enhance your success and broaden your appeal, Whispering Pine Press International, Inc., can help.

For more information, write, phone, or fax to:

Whispering Pine Press International, Inc.

P.O. Box 214, Spokane Valley, WA 99037-0214 USA

Phone: (509) 928-8700 | Fax: (509) 922-9949

Email: sales@WhisperingPinePress.com

Publisher Website: www.WhisperingPinePress.com

Book Website: www.OnionDelightsCookbook.com

SAN 253-200X

Personalized and/or Translated Order Form for Any Book by Whispering Pine Press International, Inc.

Dear Readers:

If you or your organization wishes to have this book or any other of our books personalized, we will gladly accommodate your needs. For instance, if you would like to change the names of the characters in a book to the names of the children in your family or Sunday school class, we would be happy to work with you on such a project. We can add more information of your choosing and customize this book especially for your family, group, or organization.

We are also offering an option of translating your book into another language. Please fill out the form below telling us exactly how you would like us to personalize your book.

Please send your request to:

Whispering Pine Press International, Inc.

P.O. Box 214, Spokane Valley, WA 99037-0214 USA

Phone: (509) 928-8700 | Fax: (509) 922-9949

Email: sales@WhisperingPinePress.com

Publisher Website: www.WhisperingPinePress.com

Book Website: www.OnionDelightsCookbook.com

Person/Organization placing request: ____________________

Date__________ Phone: (___) ____________________

Address____________________ Fax: (___)__________

City__________ State_____ Zip: __________

Language of the book: ____________________

Please explain your request in detail: ____________________

____

____

____

____

____

Onion Delights Cookbook

A Collection of Onion Recipes

How to Order

Get your additional copies of this book by returning an order form and your check, money order, or credit card information to:

Whispering Pine Press International, Inc.

P.O. Box 214, Spokane Valley, WA 99037-0214 USA

Phone: (509) 928-8700 | Fax: (509) 922-9949

Email: sales@WhisperingPinePress.com

Publisher Website: www.WhisperingPinePress.com

Book Website: www.OnionDelightsCookbook.com

Customer Name: ______________________________

Address: ______________________________

City, St., Zip: ______________________________

Phone/Fax: ______________________________

Email: ______________________________

- -

Please send me _____ copies of ________________ ______________________________ at $_______ per copy and $4.95 for shipping and handling per book, plus $2.95 each for additional books. Enclosed is my check, money order, or charge my account for $____________.

☐ Check ☐ Money Order ☐ Credit Card

(*Circle One*) MasterCard | Discover | Visa | American Express

☐☐☐☐ ☐☐☐☐ ☐☐☐☐ ☐☐☐☐

Expiration Date: ________________

____

Signature

____

Print Name

Whispering Pine Press International, Inc. Order Form

Gift-wrapping, Autographing, and Inscription

We are proud to offer personal autographing by the author. For a limited time this service is absolutely free! Gift-wrapping is also available for $4.95 per item.

1. Sold To

Name: ____________________

Street/Route: ____________________

____

City: ____________________

State: __________ Zip: __________

Country: ____________________

Gift message: ____________________

____

Email address: ____________________

Daytime Phone: (_ _ _) _ _ _-_ _ _ _

*Necessary for verifying orders

Home Phone: (_ _ _) _ _ _-_ _ _ _

Fax: (_ _ _) _ _ _-_ _ _ _

2. Ship To

☐ Is this a new or corrected address?

☐ Alternative Shipping Address

☐ Mailing Address

Name: ____________________

Address: ____________________

____

City: ____________________

State: __________ Zip: __________

Country: ____________________

Email address: ____________________

3. Items Ordered

ISBN # /Item #	Size	Color	Qty.	Title or Description	Price	Total

4. Method Of Payment

International, Inc. (No Cash or COD's)

☐ Visa ☐ MasterCard ☐ Discover ☐ American Express ☐ Check/Money Order

Please make it payable to Whispering Pine Press International, Inc. (No Cash or COD's)

Account Number

☐☐☐☐ ☐☐☐☐ ☐☐☐☐ ☐☐☐☐

Expiration Date

_____ / _____

Month Year

Signature____________________

Cardholder's signature

Printed Name____________________

Please print name of cardholder

Address of Cardholder____________________

Subtotal	
Gift wrap $4.95 Each	
For delivery in WA add 8.7% sales tax.	
Shipping See chart at left	
6. Total	

5. Shipping & Handling

Continental US

US Postal Ground: For books please add $4.95 for the first book and $2.95 each for additional books.

All non-book items, add 15% of the Subtotal.

Please allow 1-4 weeks for delivery.

US Postal Air: Please add $15.00 shipping and handling.

Please allow 1-3 days for delivery.

Alaska, Hawaii, and the US Territories By Ship:

Please add 10% shipping and handling (minimum charge $15.00).

Please

By Air: Please add 12% shipping and handling (minimum charge $15.00).

Please allow 2 –6 weeks for delivery.

International By Ship: Please add 10% shipping and handling (minimum charge $15.00).

Please allow 6-12 weeks for delivery.

By Air: Please add 12% shipping and handling (minimum charge $15.00).

Please allow 2-6 weeks for delivery.

FedEx Shipments: Add $5.00 to the above airmail charges for overnight delivery.

Shop Online:

www.whisperingpinepress.com

Fax orders to: (509) 922-9949

Whispering Pine Press International, Inc.

P.O. Box 214

Spokane Valley, WA 99037-0214 USA

Phone: (509) 928-8700 • Fax: (509) 922-9949

Email: sales@whisperingpinepress.com

Website: www.whisperingpinepress.com

About the Author and Cook

Karen Jean Matsko Hood has always enjoyed cooking, baking, and experimenting with recipes. At this time Hood is working to complete a series of cookbooks that blends her skills and experience in cooking and entertaining. Hood entertains large groups of people and especially enjoys designing creative menus with holiday, international, ethnic, and regional themes.

Hood is publishing a cookbook series entitled the Cookbook Delights Series, in which each cookbook emphasizes a different food ingredient or theme. The first cookbook in the series is Apple Delights Cookbook. Hood is working to complete another series of cookbooks titled Hood and Matsko Family Cookbooks, which includes many recipes handed down from her family heritage and others that have emerged from more current family traditions. She has been invited to speak on talk radio shows on various topics, and favorite recipes from her cookbooks have been prepared on local television programs.

Hood was born and raised in Great Falls, Montana. As an undergraduate, she attended the College of St. Benedict in St. Joseph, Minnesota, and St. John's University in Collegeville, Minnesota. She attended the University of Great Falls in Great Falls, Montana. Hood received a B.S. Degree in Natural Science from the College of St. Benedict and minored in both Psychology and Secondary Education. Upon her graduation, Hood and her husband taught science and math on the island of St. Croix in the U.S. Virgin Islands. Hood has completed postgraduate classes at the University of Iowa in Iowa City, Iowa. In May 2001, she completed her Master's Degree in Pastoral Ministry at Gonzaga University in Spokane, Washington. She has taken postgraduate classes at Lewis and Clark College on the North Idaho college campus in Coeur d'Alene, Idaho, Taylor University in Fort Wayne, Indiana, Spokane Falls Community College, Spokane Community College, Washington State University, University of Washington, and Eastern Washington University. Hood is working on research projects to complete her Ph.D. in Leadership Studies at Gonzaga University in Spokane, Washington.

Hood resides in Greenacres, Washington, along with her husband, many of her sixteen children, and foster children. Her interests include writing, research, and teaching. She previously has volunteered as a court advocate in the Spokane juvenile court system for abused and neglected children. Hood is a literary advocate for youth and adults. Her hobbies include cooking, baking, collecting, photography, indoor and outdoor gardening, farming, and the cultivation of unusual flowering plants and orchids. She enjoys raising several specialty breeds of animals including Babydoll Southdown, Friesen, and Icelandic sheep, Icelandic horses, bichons frisés, cockapoos, Icelandic sheepdogs, a Newfoundland, a Rottweiler, a variety of Nubian and fainting goats, and a few rescue cats. Hood also enjoys bird-watching and finds all aspects of nature precious.

She demonstrates a passionate appreciation of the environment and a respect for all life. She also invites you to visit her websites:

www.KarenJeanMatskoHood.com
www.KarenJeanMatskoHoodBookstore.com
www.KarenJeanMatskoHoodBlog.com
www.KarensKidsBooks.com
www.KarensTeenBooks.com

www.HoodFamilyBlog.com
www.HoodFamily.com

Author's Social Media

Please Follow the Author on **Twitter:** @KarenJeanHood
Friend her on **Facebook:** Karen Jean Matsko Hood Author Fan Page
Google Plus Profile: Karen Jean Matsko Hood
Pinterest.com/KarenJMHood